The Funding CRISIS
in State Unemployment Insurance

Wayne Vroman
The Urban Institute

1986

W. E. Upjohn Institute for Employment Research

Library of Congress Cataloging in Publication Data

Vroman, Wayne.
  The funding crisis in state unemployment insurance.

  Bibliography: p.
  1. Insurance, Unemployment—United States.
  I. Title.
HD7096.U5V76   1986   353.9'38256   86-1626
ISBN 0-88099-035-X
ISBN 0-88099-034-1

THE INSTITUTE, a nonprofit research organization, was established on July 1, 1945. It is an activity of the W. E. Upjohn Unemployment Trustee Corporation, which was formed in 1932 to administer a fund set aside by the late Dr. W. E. Upjohn for the purpose of carrying on "research into the causes and effects of unemployment and measures for the alleviation of unemployment."

The Author

Dr. Wayne Vroman is a senior research associate at The Urban Institute. He has directed several research projects and published widely on such topics as money wage inflation, employment discrimination, payroll tax incidence, retirement behavior and permanent partial disability. In earlier research on unemployment insurance he developed a microsimulation model of benefit payments in the individual state programs. He has also examined a number of other unemployment insurance subjects such as the program's macroeconomic effects, replacement rates, legislative developments and program performance in the first half of the 1980s.

Foreword

Severe and lengthy recessions since 1970 have left many state unemployment insurance (UI) programs with problems of insolvency and debt. The federal-state system of unemployment insurance was intended to be a self-financing social insurance program in which states levied payroll taxes on covered employers and paid benefits to eligible workers. Because benefit outlays have been exceeding tax revenues, however, there has been a widespread loss of trust fund reserves, large scale borrowing, and substantial debt accumulation. Although the volume of borrowing and aggregate indebtedness have started to decline in the mid-1980s, it is likely that indebtedness will persist in some states and that trust fund reserves will remain unacceptably low for most of the decade.

In reviewing the history of funding problems in unemployment insurance since World War II, Dr. Vroman focuses on the period from 1970 to 1983, with emphasis on those states where funding problems have been most severe. He also analyzes recent debtor state adjustments, along with conditions associated with debt avoidance, and offers his findings as a basis for insights into why the problems have arisen and what policy issues should be considered.

Facts and observations expressed in this study are the sole responsibility of the author. His viewpoints do not necessarily represent positions of the W. E. Upjohn Institute for Employment Research.

Robert G. Spiegelman
Executive Director

February 1986

v

Preface

In the mid-1980s, the federal-state system of unemployment insurance in the U.S. appears to be recovering from financial problems experienced during the 1970s and the back-to-back recessions of 1980 and 1981-82. During 1984 and 1985, the volume of borrowing by debtor states fell, loan repayments increased measurably and aggregate indebtedness declined. From an actuarial perspective, however, the conditon of the system is still very poor. Even if the current economic recovery proceeds at a brisk pace for the rest of the decade, it is not likely that trust fund reserves will be rebuilt to a level that satisfies accepted actuarial standards. Indebtedness is likely to persist in several major northern industrial states for most of the decade. The onset of a new recession could trigger a repetition of borrowing activities and debt accumulation that occurred during 1980-83.

The present volume focuses on the recent history of financing problems in unemployment insurance. It reviews post-World War II experiences, emphasizing the period from 1970 to 1983. Chapter 1 provides an overview of the funding problem. Chapter 2 is devoted mainly to analyses of the individual states where funding problems have been most serious. It also includes a cross-state analysis of recent debtor state adjustments. Chapter 3 focuses on some of the conditions associated with debt avoidance. To the extent that there are success stories in the system of unemployment insurance programs, they are contained in this chapter. The volume is intended to document recent funding problems in this established program of social insurance and to provide insights into why the problems have arisen. Although it does not offer a prescription for avoiding future funding problems, a concluding section does briefly discuss some relevant policy issues.

Acknowledgments

This work could not have been completed without the help of several other persons with a strong interest and detailed understanding of state unemployment insurance programs. Although I have not made all of the changes suggested by readers of a preliminary draft, their comments have been most helpful in the preparation of this document. I would like to thank them and add the usual caveats about remaining errors of fact and/or interpretation being my responsibility. As a careful and helpful reader of the entire manuscript, a special debt is due to Saul Blaustein of the Upjohn Institute. His comments have influenced all parts of this volume. For providing unpublished data appearing in several tables, I thank Jim Manning and those of his staff at the Unemployment Insurance Service of the U.S. Labor Department: Cindy Ambler, Harold Rice and Shelia Woodard. Several people in individual states helped me in different ways that included providing data, describing recent state-level developments and reviewing draft descriptions of their state's experiences. A short list of those persons includes Carl Brewster, Jim Hemmerly, Daniel Light, Robert Malooly, Cliff Miller, Eugene Sampson, Bill Schwarz, Tom West, Alan Williamson and Earl Wright. Finally, the Upjohn Institute is thanked not only for the financial support that made this project possible but also for a continuing demonstration of interest in unemployment insurance.

CONTENTS

List of Tables

1
The Funding Problem

State unemployment insurance (UI) programs have recently been experiencing financial problems of a magnitude unprecedented in their entire history. A series of severe and lengthy recessions since 1970 has caused benefit payments to exceed tax revenues by wide margins in many years, depleted trust fund balances and forced several states to borrow large amounts from the federal loan fund account in the Unemployment Trust Fund. During calendar year 1983, 27 states borrowed a total of $6.6 billion. The total outstanding debt at the end of the year was $13.3 billion.[1] During 1984, a year of strong economic growth, state indebtedness was reduced but still remained at $9.5 billion on December 31, 1984.

State UI programs, created in the 1930s,[2] were intended to be self-financing social insurance programs that levied payroll taxes on covered employers and paid benefits to eligible unemployed workers. Typical beneficiaries are laid-off workers who satisfy other eligibility criteria, e.g., they have sufficient employment or earnings prior to unemployment, are able to work, and available for work. Workers collect UI benefits for a limited time period until they are recalled, find another job, leave the labor force, or exhaust their benefits. Maximum regular benefit duration allowed under state laws is usually 26 weeks or less, but the actual duration of benefits drawn per claimant has typically averaged from 12 to 16 weeks during the last 10 years.

A unique feature of UI programs is their method of taxation.[3] The original authorizing legislation (Title IX of the 1935 Social Security Act) provided for a Federal Unemployment Tax (or FUT) that was to equal 3 percent of payroll in covered employment and to be paid by all covered employers. The legislation also provided for a tax offset for state UI taxes paid, up to 90 percent of the FUT or 2.7 percent of payroll for employers in states that established acceptable UI programs. If employers paid UI taxes to the state at a rate of less than 2.7 percent, they could still receive full credit for the maximum FUT tax offset provided their reduced state tax rate was based on experience. Thus the net FUT tax rate which employers paid to the federal government was .3 percent. Originally the UI payroll taxes were levied on total payroll, but in 1940 the taxable wage base was set at $3,000 per employee to correspond with the wage base under the OASI (or Social Security) program.

This general arrangement for federal and state UI taxes has continued down to the present. In 1984, the net FUT tax rate was levied at a rate of .8 percent of taxable payrolls (wages up to $7,000 per covered employee), after the tax offset of 2.7 percent for state UI taxes. In 1985 the same net FUT rate continues to be in force, but the maximum offset doubles to 5.4 percent. Each state UI program must have a maximum tax rate of at least 5.4 percent.[4] Thus, between 1938 and 1985, the net FUT tax rate has increased from .3 to .8 percent of taxable payroll, the gross FUT rate has increased from 3.0 to 6.2 percent and the tax offset has increased from 2.7 to 5.4 percent. The taxable wage base, set at $3,000 in 1940, is $7,000 in 1985.

State UI programs are influenced by both federal and state legislation. The individual states determine their own eligibility criteria, weekly benefit levels, and the number of weeks of benefits payable. In most states, weekly benefits are

50 to 60 percent of previous wages, but subject to a weekly benefit maximum. Maximum regular benefit duration payable is usually 26 weeks.

The UI payroll taxes levied by the states on covered employers are deposited in the Unemployment Trust Fund in the U.S. Treasury and credited to individual state trust fund accounts. The states draw on these accounts to make benefit payments. The federal unemployment tax revenues, now .8 percent of taxable payroll, are paid directly to the U.S. Treasury, and then allocated to various federal accounts in the Unemployment Trust Fund. This component of revenue (the Federal Unemployment Tax or FUT) pays for federal and state UI administrative costs, including the UI-related costs of the U.S. Employment Service (ES). Since 1970, a portion of FUT revenues has been allocated to finance the federal share of extended benefit (EB) costs. Between 1970 and 1983, the FUT tax rate has increased to pay for higher EB costs and increased costs of UI administration.[5]

The employer payroll taxes imposed by the states to finance program benefits are experienced rated. Under experience rating, benefit payments made to former employees and to workers on temporary layoff are a major determinant of employer taxes. Experience rating was intended to reduce labor turnover by making employers financially liable for layoffs. Those with fewer layoffs pay less taxes. In practice, covered employers are only partially experience rated so that the cost of a given layoff may not be fully borne by the employer who initiates the layoff. Thus, an important fraction of state UI taxes (often up to half) is raised by flat rate levies applied to all covered employers. As with benefits, employer tax rates are determined by state legislation (although the minimum tax base per employee and the maximum statutory employer tax rates are influenced by federal legislation).

State UI programs are supposed to be fully self-financed. Trust fund balances act as cushions in financing benefit payments during recessions. After being drawn down, they are to be rebuilt in subsequent economic expansions when experienced rated employer taxes rise.

The actual management of state UI trust fund balances has departed substantially from the preceding description. In fact, there has been a rather steady erosion of UI trust funds dating from the late 1940s. During the 1970s, a financing problem in state UI became apparent, and it has become an even more serious problem in the present decade. Between 1972 and 1979, 23 of the 51 "state" programs (including D.C.)[6] needed federal loans to continue payments for regular state UI benefits and the state share of extended benefits. From January 1, 1980 to December 31, 1984, more than $17.9 billion in loans were disbursed among 32 jurisdictions. Altogether, 38 states have borrowed at least once between 1972 and December 1984.

The state UI funding problem is the result of several distinct and identifiable factors. (1) The economy has experienced four separate recessions since 1969: in 1970-71, 1974-75, 1980 and 1981-82. Two of the recessions (1974-75 and 1981-82) were especially severe by historic standards. Frequent and severe economic downturns have caused very heavy demands for benefits between 1970 and 1983. (2) The recessions of the mid-1970s and the 1980s have had an unusual regional composition. States in the Northeast and Midwest have experienced worse unemployment problems than other states. As a result, the most serious funding problems have been concentrated in the so-called frost belt states. (3) Indexing for wage changes was introduced into many state programs in an asymmetrical manner during the 1960s and the 1970s. The benefit side was indexed to average wages while the taxable wage base was not indexed and changed only infrequently, e.g., the wage base for the Federal

Unemployment Tax increased only in 1972, 1978 and 1983. As a result, tax revenues have tended to grow more slowly than benefit payments. The taxable wages that support the program now represent less than half of total wages in covered employment. (4) The scope of employer-financed benefit payments was broadened in 1970 with the creation of the Federal-State Extended Benefit (EB) program. Because of the high average rate of unemployment since 1972, benefit payouts under EB have exceeded original expectations. More details about each of these four contributing factors will be discussed later in this chapter under "Origins of the Funding Problem."

Trust Fund Balances and Loans to State UI Programs

Long Term Trust Fund Decline

Table 1-1 illustrates with aggregate data the funding situation for state UI programs over the post-World War II period. The seven years that are identified are years immediately prior to recessions. End of year aggregate trust fund balances for these years (column 1) ranged from $6.7 to $12.6 billion. In absolute magnitude the 1979 balance was not a great deal larger than the 1948 balance and less than that of 1953. Column 2 shows that as a percentage of covered wages and salaries the fund balance declined from 7.9 in 1948 to .9 percent in 1979.

Columns 3, 4 and 5 provide information on the benefit potential that the trust fund balances represent. The average benefit paid for a week of total unemployment appears in column 3. Weekly benefit levels that grew by about half between 1948 and 1959 and again between 1959 and 1969, nearly doubled between 1969 and 1979. High inflation coupled with indexation combined to produce rapid growth in weekly benefit levels during the 1970s. Average potential regular

Table 1-1
Aggregate State UI Trust Fund Balances and Related Measures
Pre-Recession Years 1948 to 1979[a]

| Year | End-of-year net trust fund balance | | Average weekly benefit paid ($) | Average potential benefit duration (weeks)[b] | Fund capacity at average entitlement (millions of persons) | Average covered employment (millions) | Person years-to-employment ratio |
| | Amount ($ millions) | Percent of total covered payrolls | | | (1)/(3)x(4) | | (5)/(6) |
	(1)	(2)	(3)	(4)	(5)	(6)	(7)
1948	7,603	7.9	19.03	21.1	18.94	33.08	.572
1953	8,913	6.4	23.58	22.1	17.10	36.67	.466
1957	8,659	5.0	28.17	23.4	13.14	39.67	.331
1959	6,674	3.6	30.41	23.6	9.30	39.54	.235
1969	12,550	3.4	46.17	24.4	11.14	52.36	.213
1973	10,845	2.1	59.00	24.3	7.56	59.91	.126
1979	8,623	0.9	89.67	24.0	4.01	71.35	.056

SOURCE: Columns 1, 2, 3, 4 and 6 are from U.S. Department of Labor, *Unemployment Insurance Financial Data (1984)*. Columns 5 and 7 are based on other data in the table.

a. Data exclude Puerto Rico and the Virgin Islands.

b. Payable under state regular benefit provisions, excluding federal-state shared extended benefits.

benefit duration (excluding extended benefits) for claimants (column 4) also has grown since 1948, but since 1969 it has remained close to 24 weeks.

Column 5 then shows the implications of growth in average weekly payment levels and potential duration on the benefit capacity of the trust fund balances. In 1948, the $7,603 million year-end balance could have financed benefits for nearly 19 million persons at average total benefit entitlement levels that year. By 1979 the trust fund could cover only 4 million persons at such levels, less than one-fourth of the 1948 capacity, so measured.

A proxy for the potential unemployment risk exposure of state UI is the level of covered employment. Between 1948 and 1979 it more than doubled, rising from 33 to 71 million (column 6). Thus, while the real level of the aggregate trust fund balance declined sharply, the potential volume of claims increased. Combined, these developments meant that the benefit cushion in the trust fund declined very dramatically over this time period. Column 7 expresses this cushion, as measured in column 5, as the fraction of annual covered employment that could be compensated by the existing trust fund. It fell from .572 to .056 during these 32 years. Thus, the ability of state UI programs to provide compensation benefits without immediate resort to higher employer taxes or emergency loans has declined in a precipitous manner over the post-World War II period. The real trust fund benefit cushion at the end of 1979 was about one-tenth of its 1948 level.

Perhaps the most interesting feature of table 1-1 is the steady downtrend in the trust fund reserve position as indicated in columns 2 and 7. The only noticeable slowdown in the long term downtrend occurred between 1959 and 1969. Most of this decade was characterized by steady and substantial economic growth. Even though the 1959 reserves had been depleted by the 1958 recession, they still were somewhat more adequate than reserves 10 years later. If the 1969 aggregate trust fund balance was adequate, the 1979 balance clearly was not. The small cushion represented by the 1979 trust fund has been a major contributing factor behind the recent loans and the current indebtedness of the state UI programs.

With the full benefit of hindsight, it can be inferred that trust fund balances in the late 1940s were excessive for the needs of the program. Two ways to reduce excessive balances were through experience rated tax reductions and not raising the taxable wage base. After UI trust funds became depleted in the 1970s, it has not always been easy for states to raise employer taxes. One can speculate that the earlier situation of excess reserves followed by downward tax adjustments did not serve the UI system well when it later became necessary to increase average tax rates and tax bases.

Reasonable people may disagree in defining an adequate level of state UI trust fund reserves. Factors such as the average or usual level of state unemployment, the level and availability of benefits to the unemployed and the severity of a given recession are all relevant in assessing trust fund adequacy. One measure of adequacy has been developed by a committee of the Interstate Conference of Employment Security Agencies (ICESA). Their guideline involves a comparison of the trust fund reserve to the highest total of benefits for a 12-month period with each expressed as a proportion or ratio of total covered wages. The 12-month high benefit cost ratio is based on total payrolls for the period of those costs (or a year close to that period) while the reserve ratio is based on payrolls for the latest period. The reserve ratio is expressed as a multiple of the benefit cost ratio and is to be between 1.5 and 3.0. Under this guideline, a multiple of 1.5 (representing 18 months of benefits paid in an environment of unusually high unemployment) can be termed a minimum adequate level of reserves.

Table 1-2 presents detail on the distribution of reserve ratio multiples for 51 jurisdictions (the 50 states plus the District of Columbia) in 1969, 1973 and 1979. Also shown are medians of the 51 state multiples and multiples based on aggregate U.S. data. The table shows that most of the 1969 multiples exceeded the guideline. Thirty-five were 1.5 or larger and 15 of the remaining 16 fell between 1.00 and 1.49. The only state with a ratio below 1.0 was Michigan. In 1973, 21 state multiples exceeded 1.5 while 18 were less than 1.0. Of the 18, however, note that just 4 state ratios fell below .50. By 1979, only 2 state ratios exceeded 1.5 while 9 were negative and another 29 fell between 0 and .99. Using the 1.5 reserve ratio multiple guideline, the state systems went from a situation of at least minimum fund adequacy in 35 jurisdictions down to just 2 jurisdictions between 1969 and 1979.

For many states, the 1979 reserve ratio multiples in table 1-2 utilize data on benefit costs from the 1974-75 recession. Since that recession was unusually long and severe, it is instructive to note the distribution of reserve ratio multiples based on pre-1974 benefit cost experiences. The bottom line in the table shows these ratios for 1979. Although they are larger in several states, only 5 equal or exceed 1.5 while 31 are still smaller than 1.0. Thus, widespread reserve inadequacy is still present even when benefit experiences from pre-1974 recessions are used in the reserve ratio multiple calculations.

Based on the preceding, two broad statements about state UI trust fund balances can be made. (1) Aggregate data show clearly that between 1948 and 1979 the program evolved from a situation of trust fund overabundance to inadequacy. The measure of fund adequacy developed in column 7 in table 1-1, the ratio of person years of benefits to covered

Table 1-2

State UI Reserve Ratio Multiples in 1969, 1973 and 1979

Year	Number of states: reserve ratio as multiple of highest 12-month benefit cost ratio							Median state ratio	Ratio for U.S.
	Negative	0-.49	.50-.99	1.00-1.49	1.50-1.99	2.00-2.99	3.00 and above		
1969	0	0	1	15	14	13	8	1.84	1.68
1973	2	2	14	12	13	7	1	1.31	1.04
1979	9	12	17	11	2	0	0	.63	.41
1979 with pre-1974 benefit experience[a]	9	10	12	15	4	1	0	.77	.44

SOURCE: Based on data in U.S. Department of Labor, *Unemployment Insurance Financial Data* (1984). Reserve ratio multiples are based on reserves measured at the end of the indicated years. Medians were computed at The Urban Institute.

a. Cost ratios used in computing reserve ratio multiples are based on the highest benefit cost experiences for the years prior to 1974.

employment, reached a level in 1979 that was about one-tenth the size of its 1948 level. The critical period in this evolution was the years following 1969 when state reserve ratio multiples fell to levels that were generally below a suggested actuarial standard of 1.5. (2) The decline in trust fund reserves has been widespread and not confined to just a few states. Using the 1.5 minimum reserve ratio multiple guideline, the number of jurisdictions with inadequate trust fund reserves increased from 16 in 1969 to 49 in 1979. Widespread deficits, emergency federal loans and large debts are all direct consequences of inadequate state UI program funding.

Because funding has been inadequate, most UI programs have had to borrow at least once in the past decade. Of the 51 "states," i.e., the 50 plus the District of Columbia, 23 borrowed sometime in the 1970s while 32 borrowed sometime between January 1, 1980 and December 31, 1984. Altogether 38 different states have borrowed at least once between 1972 and December 1984.[7] Over these 13 years a total of $23.4 billion was lent to insolvent state UI programs.

Although the present study focuses primarily on state fund insolvency and debt, one has to recognize the diversity of individual state experiences. Several states have never become insolvent while others have borrowed only relatively small amounts for brief periods. The programs that have been successful in avoiding major funding problems are examined in chapter 3. Despite the diversity of state experiences, it must be emphasized that the loss of fund adequacy has been a pervasive phenomenon. Only two states entered the 1980s with reserve ratio multiples of at least 1.5. Even after all UI indebtedness is eliminated, it will require substantial additional trust fund rebuilding to achieve a distribution of reserve ratio multiples approaching that which existed at the end of 1969. In other words, a long-run solvency problem will continue to exist even after all current indebtedness has been eliminated.

Trust Fund Insolvency and Debt

Table 1-3 displays aggregate annual data on loan activities and indebtedness since 1969. Columns 1 and 2 respectively show the start-of-year trust fund position of the programs (more precisely the reserve ratio multiple) and the annual unemployment rate for the civilian labor force. Because the 1974-75 recession followed closely after the 1970-71 downturn, very little trust fund rebuilding occurred in 1972 and 1973. As a consequence, benefit payments associated with the very high unemployment rates of 1975-77 caused a precipitous decline in the aggregate reserve ratio multiple and loans were required by many state UI programs. Loans of $4.5 billion were made in 1975-77 and for the entire 1972-79 period the total was $5.5 billion. Substantial loan repayments occurred in 1979, but $3.7 billion of debt remained at the end of that year as the economy entered another major recessionary period.

The recession of 1980 seriously impacted state UI programs whose trust funds were even more depleted than they had been in 1974-75. About $3.1 billion was borrowed in 1980-81. When unemployment then rose to even higher levels in 1982 and 1983, annual loans of $5.2 billion and $6.6 billion were required. More than half (27) of the state UI programs had to borrow in 1983. With practically nonexistent trust fund cushions large benefit payouts meant an immediate need for federal loans. State borrowing in 1983 equaled about one-third of all benefit payments made under regular state UI and EB programs.

The year 1983 was noteworthy not only for the amount of loans but also for the volume of loan repayments. The $3.9 billion of repayments was nearly three times the amount repaid in 1979, the second highest previous repayment year. A heavy volume of loan repayments occurred despite the fact that 1983 was a year of serious recession. Loan repayments

Table 1-3
Summary Data on State UI Trust Fund Adequacy, Loans, Loan Repayments and Debt, U.S., 1969 to 1984

Year	Start-of-year reserve ratio multiple (1)	Unemployment rate (percent) (2)	States requiring loans (number) (3)	Loans ($millions) (4)	Loan repayments ($millions) (5)	End-of-year debt ($millions) (6)	End-of-year states in debt (number) (7)
1969	1.72	3.5	0	0	0	0	0
1970	1.68	4.9	0	0	0	0	0
1971	1.51	5.9	0	0	0	0	0
1972	1.18	5.6	1	32	0	32	1
1973	1.00	4.9	2	62	0	94	2
1974	1.04	5.6	3	17	0	111	3
1975	.92	8.5	14	1,456	13	1,554	14
1976	.24	7.7	21	1,827	36	3,345	20
1977	.06	7.1	18	1,265	110	4,500	20
1978	.06	6.1	10	826	337	4,989	16
1979	.25	5.8	3	46	1,307	3,728	11
1980	.41	7.1	8	1,471	305	4,894	14
1981	.29	7.6	9	1,614	321	6,187	15
1982	.23	9.7	16	5,187	813	10,561	21
1983	-.10	9.6	27	6,632	3,914	13,279	21
1984	-.20	7.5	18	3,005	6,826	9,452	17

SOURCE: Data in columns (1), (6) and (7) taken from U.S. Department of Labor, *Unemployment Insurance Financial Data* (1984). Column (2) taken from U.S. Executive Office of the President, *Economic Report of the President* (1984). Columns (4) and (5) are based on unpublished data from the U.S. Department of Labor. All data refer to the 50 states plus the District of Columbia.

totaling $6.8 billion took place in 1984. Since the recent loans are interest-bearing, debtor states have been repaying them at a particularly rapid rate. Over 80 percent of total loan repayments in both 1983 and 1984 were made on interest-bearing debt. In contrast, loan repayments were of minor importance during 1975-77, the years of highest unemployment during the 1970s. Because of these recent repayments end-of-year indebtedness grew by only $2.7 billion (from $10.6 to $13.3 billion) between 1982 and 1983, while it declined by about $3.8 billion between 1983 and 1984. To better understand why large repayments occurred in a year of such high unemployment it will be useful to describe the repayment provisions of the federal laws, the costs of indebtedness and how these costs have increased in the 1980s.

Repayment of loans by the states can be made in two ways. (1) States can make voluntary payments from their trust fund accounts to the federal loan account. (2) Employers in debtor states may be subject to increased taxes under the Federal Unemployment Tax. As noted earlier, the basic net FUT rate is .8 percent. For states with outstanding loans, however, the FUT net rate is automatically raised by predetermined amounts and the proceeds are used to repay debts. These higher taxes can be termed FUT penalty taxes.

Penalty taxes are applied after a state loan has been outstanding on January 1 of two consecutive years. The penalty tax rate is .3 percent of federally taxable payroll in the first year of applicability and it rises by increments of .3 percent in subsequent years[8] until the outstanding loan is fully repaid. (The FUT rate increases are really reductions in the amount of the tax credit allowed. Thus, the full tax offset of 2.7 percent prior to 1985 was reduced to 2.4, then to 2.1, and so on. After 1984, the full offset of 5.4 percent is reduced to 5.1, 4.8, etc.). Connecticut was the first state to need federal loans (March 1972 was the first loan date), and its employers were subject to a .3 percent FUT penalty tax payable in 1975 (based on 1974 taxable wages).

Altogether, a total of 23 different states secured loans in the 1970s, but only 7 actually paid penalty taxes prior to 1980.[9] Full implementation of the penalty tax provisions was twice deferred by legislation during the 1970s. Because it was viewed as inappropriate to impose penalty taxes in a period of high unemployment and low employer profits, federal amendments of the repayment provisions were enacted in 1975 (PL94-45) and 1977 (PL95-19) that deferred until 1978 and then until 1980 the full applicability of the penalty tax provisions. The loans made during the 1970s were not financially onerous for the debtor states for another reason. There were no interest charges on the outstanding debt.

Individual debtor states followed a variety of policies in repaying the loans. By the end of 1979, 12 of the 23 that had borrowed had completely paid off their loans by transfer from their reserve accounts, and 2 more completed their debt repayments during 1980.[10] Although 12 of the 23 debtor states had fully repaid their loans by the end of 1979, about two-thirds of the principal ($3.7 of $5.5 billion) remained outstanding. Of the $3.7 billion debt, $3.2 billion was concentrated in just four states (Connecticut - $.4 billion; Illinois - $.9 billion; New Jersey - $.7 billion; and Pennsylvania - $1.2 billion). Besides these states, the other five that continued in debt past 1980 were Delaware, the District of Columbia, Maine, Rhode Island and Vermont. These states did little or nothing to repay their loans, even though the bulk of the lending occurred prior to 1978.[11] Because of inflation, each year of repayment deferral reduced the real burden of their indebtedness.

The failure of some debtor states to make substantial loan repayments in the late 1970s was an important consideration in subsequent federal legislative actions. First, a further deferral of FUT penalty taxes was not seriously considered in 1979 and the penalty took effect in nine states in 1980. The dollar amount of FUT penalty taxes rose from $60 million in 1979 to over $300 million in 1980.[12] Second, the Reagan Administration in 1981 proposed that future loans would carry interest charges. This proposal was adopted as part of the Omnibus Budget Reconciliation Act of August 1981 (PL97-35). New loans made after March 31, 1982 carry an annual interest charge if not fully repaid within the same fiscal year. Interest was charged on the average outstanding loan balance, and the interest rate was the same as the rate paid on state UI trust fund investments (but subject to a maximum rate of 10 percent per year).[13] Combined, these interest and FUT penalty applications meant that future loans would be more expensive and debt repayment would be more prompt.[14]

The 1981 Omnibus Budget Reconciliation Act also contained provisions to limit FUT penalty taxes. Four solvency requirements were listed that, if met by a state, could limit the penalty taxes applicable during the years 1981 to 1987. The four requirements were: (1) to maintain unemployment tax effort; (2) not to reduce net solvency in the program; (3) to have the tax rate (based on total wages) at least equal the prior five-year average benefit cost rate; and (4) to avoid increases in total indebtedness after 1981.[15] The last two requirements were applicable starting in 1983. States could limit FUT penalty taxes in 1981 and 1982 merely by not lowering employer taxes and not raising benefits or easing benefit eligibility. The FUT penalty rate was limited to .6 percent or to the pre-1981 rate if it exceeded .6 percent. Since FUT penalty taxes are payable in January of the year after they accrue, this legislation meant that a .6 percent penalty tax was levied in eight states in January 1982 and only in Connecticut was it higher.

The economic downturn of 1981-82, however, led to a renewed concern about the financial problems confronting debtor states. As unemployment increased in late 1981 and throughout 1982, it became clear that the higher costs of debt repayment would be experienced while the states were in the midst of a very severe recession. The Tax Equity and Fiscal Responsibility Act of 1982 (PL97-248, also known as TEFRA) contained provisions designed to lessen recession-induced economic hardships both for workers with long term unemployment and for state UI programs with financing problems. A program of Federal Supplemental Compensation (FSC) was created to provide extra weeks of long term benefits to workers exhausting their regular state UI or EB entitlements.[16]

Important TEFRA provisions focused on financing and debt repayment issues. (1) The Federal Unemployment Tax was modified in several ways. Starting in 1983, the taxable wage base was raised from $6,000 to $7,000 per covered workers and the net tax rate was increased from .7 to .8 percent of taxable wages. Also the gross federal UI tax rate was raised from 3.5 to 6.2 percent starting in 1985. This change doubles the maximum credit allowed employers for state UI taxes from 2.7 to 5.4 percent since the net FUT rate remains at .8. State tax rates may not be less than 5.4 except through experience rating and maximum state tax rates still less than 5.4 will have to rise to at least that level.

(2) Starting in 1983, debtor states could avoid FUT penalty taxes for their employers. To avoid these taxes, a state must (i) repay current year advances before November 10, (ii) pay from its reserves an amount toward reducing its prior debt equivalent to the potential penalty taxes, (iii) have a trust fund balance on November 1 equal to at least three months worth of benefits and (iv) enact a net increase in program solvency. Wisconsin, for example, which first obtained loans in 1982, will be able to avoid FUT penalty taxes in 1985

because it satisfies these four TEFRA financial requirements.[17]

Other TEFRA financial provisions were as follows. (3) It limited the potentially sharp increases in FUT penalty taxes (much larger than .3 percent) applicable after several years in debtor states that had not improved the financial solvency of their programs. (4) States with very high insured unemployment rates (IURs) were allowed to defer up to three-fourths of their annual interest payment due after the end of 1982. The deferred amounts were to be repaid in the subsequent three years and to accrue interest while they remained unpaid. The threshold IUR was 7.5 percent, a rate so high that only Michigan's rate for the first six months of 1982 exceeded this level.

An examination of these TEFRA financial provisions shows they were intended both to improve overall state UI program solvency and to provide partial financial relief to some debtor states. Improved program solvency would result in some states from the tax base increase in 1983, the higher gross FUT tax rate in 1985 and from inducements for states to enact legislation. Penalty taxes could be avoided if solvency was improved. Avoidance of penalty taxes by paying the equivalent from the state fund permits the state to finance the repayment through an experience rated rather than a flat rate tax.

Because unemployment continued to rise throughout 1982, the volume of new loans rose sharply and exceeded $5 billion for the year. States faced the obvious prospect of high interest charges in 1983 and later years. In fact, since market interest rates remained high throughout 1982, it was apparent that interest payments would become increasingly burdensome. The legislation of 1981 and 1982 gave the states the ability to limit their FUT penalty taxes, but they could not reduce their interest payments. In states with large debts, interest charges would soon exceed FUT penalty taxes, and high unemployment meant that increased borrowing was inevitable. The partial financial relief provided to Michigan with its unusually high IUR was not available to other states and even that relief had its price, i.e., interest accrued on the deferred interest payments.

The Social Security Amendments of March 1983 (PL98-21) contained provisions that addressed the costs of UI loans and indebtedness. For debtor state UI programs, interest and debt repayment terms were made potentially easier. If a debtor state maintained its tax effort and increased its net solvency in 1983 (or the first year of indebtedness) through tax increases and/or benefit reductions by 25 percent (and then by more in subsequent years), it would be allowed during fiscal years 1983, 1984, and 1985 to defer until later years at no cost 80 percent of the interest payments on federal loans made after March 31, 1982.[18] Interest deferrals would also be allowed if taxes as a percent of a total payroll equaled or exceeded 2 percent in calendar year 1982. Only two debtor states were eligible under this alternative interest deferral criterion: Rhode Island and West Virginia.

A second financial inducement to improve net solvency was provided in the form of potentially lower interest rates. If net solvency was improved by 50 percent in 1983 (or the first year of indebtedness), the state would be eligible for a 1 percentage point reduction in the interest rate charged on interest-bearing debt, e.g., from 10 to 9 percent for 1982 loans.[19]

The 1983 Social Security Amendments also addressed the potential costs of FUT penalty taxes. The four solvency requirements listed in the Omnibus Budget Reconciliation Act of 1981 were again introduced as criteria for limiting these taxes. In this 1983 legislation, however, any state satisfying all four requirements would be eligible for a permanent cap (as opposed to a temporary cap lasting only until 1987) on FUT penalty taxes. Also, criteria were listed for reducing annual increments in penalty tax rates (to .1 or .2 percent per year) in states where some but not all of the four requirements were met.[20] All of these provisions have the effect of allowing states to reduce and/or defer the financial obligations associated with their debts.

By charging interest on new loans, the federal government has provided the states with strong financial incentives to repay outstanding debts. If debts are repaid quickly, i.e., in the year that they are incurred, interest charges can be completely avoided. Voluntary repayments can be applied to interest-bearing debt even if the state has older debt incurred before April 1, 1982. The repayment activities of 1983 and 1984 previously noted in table 1-3 reflect this repayment behavior. Between April 1, 1982 and December 31, 1983, for example, new loans totaled $10.1 billion but only $6.4 billion was still outstanding at the end of 1983. As noted, loan repayments in the first nine months of 1984 totaled $5.9 billion. Compared to earlier periods, this is a very rapid rate of repayment, particularly considering that 1983-84 have been years of very high unemployment.

The interest costs and FUT penalty taxes when coupled with the potential financial relief provided by the 1983 Social Security Amendments give debtor states very strong inducements to modify their UI laws. Following the Amendments, legislation has been enacted or at least proposed in nearly all states with large debts. Chapter 2 will examine these legislative initiatives in some detail. Before moving on to the specifics of the changes, however, there are background issues regarding the origins of the funding crisis that need to be addressed.

Origins of the Funding Problem

The funding problem that state UI programs are currently experiencing has origins in the recent overall performance of the economy. Adverse economic developments coupled with key revenue and benefit features of UI programs have resulted in a persistent tendency for benefit payouts to exceed revenues since 1969. Four developments will be examined in subsequent paragraphs: (1) real GNP growth; (2) regional growth differentials; (3) recent inflation and (4) the Federal-State Extended Benefit (EB) program. All four have contributed to the funding problem.

Variations in Real GNP Growth Rates

Table 1-4 presents summary data on U.S. macroeconomic performance between 1949 and 1983. The starting point, 1949, is the year of the first post-World War II recession and a year when state UI programs had abundant, perhaps overabundant, trust fund reserves. Indicators in the table are organized roughly by decade with the exact time periods being 1949-59, 1960-69, 1970-79 and 1980-83. Although most are long time intervals, they do illustrate important contrasts in economic performance. The aggregate of state trust fund balances at the start of these four periods can be characterized respectively as overabundant, adequate, inadequate, and very inadequate. The aggregate reserve position, net of loans, declined sharply during the 1949-59 and the 1970-79 periods.

Annual rates of growth in the economy's output of final goods and services (real GNP) averaged just above 3 percent in the 1950s and 1970s, more than 1 full percentage point below the 4.6 percent average of the 1960s. The latter period had just one recession (1960-61) and a prolonged period of economic growth between 1961 and 1969. Due to two recessions (1980 and 1981-82) the 1980-83 period had very low real growth.

Table 1-4
Economic Performance and State UI Net Trust Fund Reserves
U.S. and Region, 1949-1983

Indicator[a] and region[b]	1949-59	1960-69	1970-79	1980-83
	Annual averages			
Real GNP growth rate	3.4	4.6	3.3	.7
Unemployment rate				
All persons 16 and older	4.6	4.8	6.2	8.5
Men 25 and older	3.6	3.1	3.6	6.3
Real labor productivity				
growth rate	2.3	2.5	1.4	1.0
Employment growth rate				
Total U.S.	1.4	2.6	2.5	-.1
North	.8	2.1	1.4	-1.0
South and West	2.4	3.3	3.8	.9
Inflation rate	2.4	2.2	6.3	7.3

Start of period net UI trust fund reserves as a percent of prior year payrolls				
Total U.S.	7.9	3.6	3.4	0.9
North	7.6	3.2	3.4	-0.1
South and West	8.5	4.2	3.5	2.0

SOURCES: Rates of GNP and labor productivity (output per man hour) growth and inflation (implicit price deflator for GNP) based on national income accounts data (for nonfarm
business sector) from U.S. Executive Office of the President, *Economic Report of the
President* (1984), table B-41, p. 267.

Unemployment rates based on monthly household survey and employment growth rates
on the establishment survey. Data taken from *Employment and Earnings* (May 1984), pp.
128/151 and earlier U.S. Department of Labor Publications.

Trust fund reserves and payrolls data from U.S. Department of Labor, *Unemployment
Insurance Financial Data* (1984).

a. Economic performance indicators are measured as percentage changes and averaged
over the indicated period; UI trust fund reserves are measured at the start of each period
and expressed as a percentage of total covered payrolls in the previous year.

b. The "North" region includes states in the North East and North Central divisions as
defined by the Census Bureau; the "South and West" includes all other states.

The effects of economic recessions are apparent not only in economic growth rates, but also in the average unemployment rates. Because high unemployment leads to increased demand for UI benefits, average unemployment rates have obvious implications for UI trust fund payouts. Since World War II the composition of U.S. unemployment has undergone a long run change with an increasing share of the total made up of younger persons and women, groups whose unemployment rates are typically higher than the rates experienced by adult men. This changing mix has tended to increase the economy's average unemployment rate in more recent years and to increase the minimum unemployment rate consistent with a full employment economy.[21] Table 1-4 illustrates the importance of this mix effect by displaying two sets of average unemployment rates; the rate for all persons 16 and older and the rate for adult men 25 and older. The adult male unemployment rate, which is more comparable across time periods, clearly illustrates the economy's superior performance of the 1960s in comparison to the adjacent earlier and later decades. Since adult men are the demographic group most likely to be UI beneficiaries, movements in their average rate provide a useful gauge of the demand for UI benefits. Both average unemployment rates are very high in the 1980-83 period.

The data on real GNP growth rates and adult male unemployment rates convey similar messages. Frequent recessions in the 1950s and 1970s caused substantial drains on UI trust fund reserves. Because the system started the 1950s with excessive reserves, however, it emerged from the 1950s with generally adequate reserves, although 12 states had less than adequate reserves, including 3 in debt. Ten years later, aggregate reserves still seemed generally adequate, but 16 states had reserve ratio multiples that fell below 1.5. The excessive reserve cushion from the late 1940s was not present at the start of the 1970s, and, as a result, the

recessions of this decade necessitated borrowing by many
state UI programs. Given the low reserves and very high
unemployment rates of 1980-83, borrowing in this latest
period has also been widespread.

Disparities in Regional Rates of Economic Growth

Output growth translates into employment growth as increased real production raises demand for labor and creates
more jobs. The association between output growth and
employment growth, however, is also influenced by labor
productivity growth. For a given rate of output growth, a
lower rate of productivity growth will imply a faster rate of
employment growth. Table 1-4 documents the slowdown in
labor productivity growth that occurred in the 1970s when
average man hour productivity grew by 1.4 percent per year
compared to averages of 2.3-2.5 percent in the preceding two
decades. Because of the productivity slowdown average
employment growth was nearly as fast in the 1970s as it had
been in the 1960s, despite the slower pace of output growth.
On average, employment grew by 2.5 percent per year in the
1970s compared to 2.6 percent in the 1960s. Since employment growth and productivity growth are very sensitive to
short-run business cycle developments, their slow growth in
1980-83 reflects cyclical factors.

Over the entire period since World War II, there have been
systematic differences in regional rates of economic growth.
States in the South and West have consistently exhibited
higher than average growth while states in the North have
grown more slowly. Table 1-4 illustrates these regional differences with data on employment growth rates. The
cumulative effect of the employment growth differentials
over this 34-year period is quite dramatic. In 1948, states in
the North had 63 percent of total U.S. employment, but by
1983 their employment share had declined to 47 percent.

Since 1970, the differences in regional growth rates have been especially pronounced. The first energy crisis of 1973-75 increased the relative costs of doing business in the North (so-called frost belt states) and hastened the pace of regional population and employment reallocations. Employment growth data in table 1-4 illustrate the increased regional disparities. As noted, employment growth for the U.S. as a whole was only .1 percent lower in the 1970s compared to the 1960s. However, employment growth during the 1970s was .7 percent lower in the North but actually .5 percent higher in the South and West when compared to the preceding decade. These wider regional disparities have persisted through the first four years of the present decade.

Given the way that UI programs are financed, increased regional growth disparities can have differential implications for trust fund balances in individual states. Consider some consequences of a company closing a plant in the North and simultaneously opening a plant in the South or West. The claims of laid-off workers are the obligation of the program in the state where the plant closure occurs. The closing will cause a loss of tax revenues as well as an increase in benefit claims. Even if the worker moves out of the state to find a new job, he or she can file an interstate claim that is the financial obligation of employers in the original state. New and expanding plants in the growing region pay taxes for new employees as soon as the workers are hired. For new plants, the employer taxes are not reduced by an experience factors so that trust fund reserves are accumulated quickly in the first few years of operation. New employees must work for a time before satisfying the monetary eligibility requirements for state UI benefits. Thus, when the regional distribution of employment changes, there is some tendency for UI trust funds to be reduced in regions that are losing employment while at the same time they are increased in regions where employment is growing.

To date there has not been a detailed study of how disparities in regional rates of economic growth affect state UI trust fund balances. It is clear from aggregate data in table 1-4, however, that employment growth disparities have been unusually wide in 1970-79 and 1980-83. It is also obvious in table 1-4 that the aggregate trust fund reserves of states in the South and West did not deteriorate as much during the 1970s as they did in the North. Reserves as a proportion of covered wages in the two regions were roughly equal in 1970; .034 in the North and .035 in the South and West. By 1980, however, reserves in the South and West were .020 of covered wages while the net reserve balance for the North as a whole was negative. In both the 1970s and in 1980-83 the bulk of loans to state UI programs has gone to states in the North.

Table 1-5 provides more detail on the regional aspect of state UI loan activities in the 1970s and in 1980-83. Column 1 displays the percentage breakdown of covered wages among the Census Bureau's four geographic regions and nine divisions. If funding problems were randomly distributed by state and region, these percentages would provide a rough guide as to how loans would be distributed. The actual percentage distributions of loans are then shown in columns 2 and 3. During the 1970s, loans were heavily concentrated in the North East with 17.6 and 41.5 percent going to New England and Middle Atlantic states respectively. Most of the remainder (28.4 percent) went to states in the East North Central division. The latter division accounted for 58.8 percent of all loans in the 1980s, a reflection of the current recession's severity in these heavily industrialized states. Thus, although states in the North were the main loan recipients in both periods, loans went mainly to Northeastern states in the 1970s and mainly to North Central states in the 1980s. Note also in columns 4 and 5 that per dollar of covered wages, New England was the largest user of loans in

Table 1-5
Federal Loans to State UI Programs
Employment Growth and Unemployment by Region

Census regions and divisions	Percent of covered wages 1979	Percent of federal loans to state UI programs		Loans as a percent of 1979 covered wages		Annual employment growth, percent		Average unemployment rate percent	
		1972-79	1980-83	1972-79	1980-83	1970-79	1980-83	1970-79	1980-83
	(1)	(2)	(3)	(4)	(5)	(6)	(7)	(8)	(9)
North East	23.1	59.1	18.5	1.5	1.3	.9	.1	7.0	8.0
New England	5.7	17.6	.6	1.8	.2	1.7	.3	6.9	6.7
Middle Atlantic	17.4	41.5	17.9	1.4	1.6	.6	-.1	7.0	8.5
North Central	28.2	31.5	65.3	.7	3.7	1.9	-1.9	5.6	9.7
East North Central	21.2	28.4	58.8	.8	4.4	1.5	-2.2	6.1	10.8
West North Central	7.0	3.1	6.5	.3	1.5	2.7	-1.1	4.2	6.9
South	28.9	5.6	14.9	.1	.8	3.7	1.0	5.5	7.9
South Atlantic	13.8	4.1	2.8	.2	.3	3.5	1.2	5.6	7.6
East South Central	5.0	1.0	2.5	.1	.8	3.3	-1.1	5.7	10.4
West South Central	10.1	.5	9.7	.0	1.5	4.2	1.9	5.2	7.0
West	19.9	3.9	1.3	.1	.1	4.0	.6	7.4	8.4
Mountain	4.5	.5	1.3	.1	.4	5.6	1.2	6.0	7.5
Pacific	15.4	3.4	0	.1	0	3.5	.4	7.8	8.8
U.S. Total - percent	100.0	100.0	100.0	--	--	--	--	--	--
U.S. Total - $ billions	934.5	5.5	14.9	.6	1.6	2.5	-.1	6.2	8.5

SOURCES: Columns (1)-(5) are based on U.S. Department of Labor, *Unemployment Insurance Financial Data* (1984) and unpublished data from the U.S. Department of Labor. Columns (6) and (7) which are based on annual averages from the Labor Department's Establishment Survey refer to non-agricultural wage and salary employment. Unemployment rates in columns (8) and (9) are based on the Labor Department-Census Bureau monthly household survey of the labor force. Data in columns (6) through (9) taken from *Employment and Earnings* (May 1984), pp. 128/151 and earlier U.S. Department of Labor publications.

the 1970s but a very minor user in the 1980s. It is clear that funding problems are now most severe in the East North Central states. All five (Ohio, Indiana, Michigan, Illinois and Wisconsin) have had to borrow in recent years.

Employment growth rates in the various regions and divisions are summarized in columns 6 and 7. As previously noted the South and West grew much faster than the national average in the 1970s (and, incidentally, even faster than their own growth rates of the 1960s) while the North East was the slowest growing region. The concentration of the 1980-83 downturn in the North Central region is indicated by the negative employment growth which is especially large in the East North Central division (–2.2 percent). Note also that New England grew faster than the national average in the 1980-83 period.

The contrasting experiences of the North East and North Central regions between 1970-79 and 1980-83 are also illustrated by the average unemployment rates in columns 8 and 9. During the 1970s, unemployment rates in the North East exceeded the national average while the East North Central division experienced roughly average rates. Their positions were exactly reversed in 1980-83 when the unemployment rate in the East North Central division was 2.3 percentage points above the national average. Especially noticeable in this period was the low unemployment in New England. Its average rate was lower than during the 1970s and 1.8 percentage points below the national average (6.7 versus 8.5 percent). It is clear from table 1-5 that in 1970-79 and again in 1980-83 loans went mainly to states in regions with high unemployment.

Following the economic downturn of 1981-82 there have been sharply higher unemployment rates in the major energy-producing states of the South (Louisiana, Oklahoma and Texas) and in (coal-producing) Kentucky and West

Virginia. For these five states, unemployment rates in 1980 were 6.7, 4.8, 5.2, 8.0 and 9.4 percent respectively. In 1983 the corresponding rates were 11.8, 9.0, 8.0, 11.7 and 18.0 percent. Because of sharp increases in unemployment four of the five energy-producing states have recently experienced UI funding problems. Louisiana and Texas borrowed $1.1 billion in 1983. Except for loans made to the State of Washington in the 1970s, these loans to Texas and Louisiana are the only large-scale advances made to states outside the North in either the 1970s or 1980-83. Table 1-5 shows that states in the West South Central division (Texas, Louisiana, and Arkansas) have accounted for 9.7 percent of total borrowing in the 1980-83 period. Although the scale of their borrowing has been generally small, it should be noted that nine southern and eight western states have had to borrow at least once since 1972.

The Pacific division contrasts with others in having both high employment growth and high unemployment, particularly during the 1970s. The absence of large-scale borrowing in this division could be evidence that high growth has favorable effects on state UI program financing. As noted above, the effects of high growth could operate either through the revenue side of the program, e.g., having more new firms contribute at a rate that exceeds their long-run average cost, or the benefit side, e.g., high growth leads to a delay in acquiring monetary eligibility and/or to less long term unemployment. Whatever the reason (or reasons), it is clear that states in the Pacific division have had fewer funding problems than states in other divisions with high unemployment.

The data in table 1-5 clearly show that UI trust fund problems have not occurred in a random manner across the economy. In both the 1970s and in 1980-83, loans have been concentrated in regions with high rates of unemployment and low rates of employment growth.

Inflation

The economy experienced much higher inflation rates in the 1970s than it did in the preceding two decades. Table 1-4, for example, shows that annual inflation rates (as measured by the implicit price deflator) averaged 2.4 and 2.2 percent during 1949-59 and 1960-69 respectively. Average inflation rates were more than twice as high in 1970-79 and 1980-83 (6.3 and 7.3 percent). The combination of both high inflation and high unemployment experienced during the 1970s was unusual, and the term stagflation became widely used to describe this situation. The OPEC oil price increases of 1973-75 and 1979-81 were an important cause for the economy's stagflation.

High rates of inflation have important implications for state UI financing. In many programs, increased wage inflation causes benefit payments to increase automatically and roughly by an amount that matches the higher inflation, while tax revenues do not keep pace. The institutional features of many programs that cause the asymmetric response are quite easy to describe. The weekly benefit maximum is often tied to an index of average earnings, e.g., the average weekly wage in manufacturing or the average for all covered employment. Thus, when inflation increases this is soon translated into higher weekly wages, a higher weekly benefit maximum and increased weekly benefits.

Indexation of the maximum weekly benefit became noticeably more widespread in the 1960s and 1970s. By 1971, half of the states had instituted indexation and 10 more followed suit later in the 1970s. In this same period there was a trend towards liberalizing the level of the maximum benefit relative to the average weekly wage. Thus, in 1971 the weekly benefit maximum equaled or exceeded 60 percent of the average weekly wage in only 8 states, but by 1983 the number had grown to 22. Both changes cause average weekly benefits to respond strongly to changes in average weekly wages.

Benefit data from the 1960s and 1970s illustrate this responsiveness. For the three years 1959, 1969, and 1979, average weekly benefits for the entire economy were $30.40, $46.17, and $89.68 respectively. The implied compound growth rate in weekly benefits over the 1960s and 1970s (4.3 and 6.9 percent respectively) exceed the inflation rates for the two decades as shown in table 1-4. When measured relative to average weekly wages in covered employment, i.e., the gross replacement rate, benefits became a somewhat larger fraction, increasing from .334 in 1959 to .344 in 1969 and then to .361 in 1979. During the 1960s and 1970s, the benefit side of UI could be described as being fully indexed. Thus when inflation increased sharply in the 1970s this meant that the financial obligation to pay benefits would have increased sharply even if unemployment rates of the 1970s had been no higher than those of the 1960s.

Increasing benefit obligations would not pose financial problems if UI tax revenues were also fully indexed to the inflation rate. Each state has an annual taxable wage base per covered employee. In most states in most years, this maximum has been the same as the taxable wage base for the Federal Unemployment Tax (FUT). Between 1940 and 1971 this maximum was $3,000 per worker. Because the federal maximum was unchanged for this long period while average wages were growing, taxable wages came to represent a smaller and smaller proportion of total wages. The ratio of taxable to total wages declined from .928 in 1940 to .453 in 1971. Several states raised their taxable wage bases above the $3,000 federal level in the 1960s and in 1970-71. The national ratio of taxable to total wages in 1971 would have been even lower than .453 had all states retained the $3,000 wage base.

During the 1960s there was an increasing recognition that the FUT taxable wage base was inadequate to finance benefits. Thus the base was raised to $4,200 in 1972 and then to $6,000 in 1978. Because of higher inflation during the

1970s, however, the ratio of taxable to total wages continued to decline. By 1982 taxable wages represented only .405 of total wages even though the wage base was twice its 1971 level. Even with an increase to $7,000 in 1983 and to higher levels in several states, taxable wages continue to represent less than half of all wages in covered employment.

Table 1-6 presents summary data on tax bases and average tax rates in state UI programs since 1960. It documents the downtrend in the ratio of taxable to total wages (column 2) and shows how the increases in the FUT maximum of 1972, 1978 and 1983 increased the ratio in those three years. Columns 3 and 4 respectively show the average tax rates on taxable wages and total wages. In the 1970s, the average rate on taxable wages did rise, but the tax rate on total wages was no higher than it was in the early 1960s. This clearly illustrates the effect of the long term downtrend in the ratio of taxable to total wages. Although average tax rates increased following the recessions of the 1970s, they did not increase enough to adequately replenish UI trust funds. Given the low taxable wage base per employee, even larger increases in statutory tax rates were needed.

Increasingly, individual states have recognized that the FUT taxable maximum is an inadequate base for employer UI taxes. Table 1-6 shows the number of states with maximums higher than the FUT maximum. By 1984, this number stood at 31. Although individual states have legislated higher maximums, they typically have not been set that much above the FUT taxable wage base. Thus, 23 states had maximums above $3,000 in 1971 but only 5 exceeded $4,200 in 1972. Note, however, after the next two tax base increases that 12 state maximums exceeded $6,000 in 1978 and then 24 exceeded $7,000 in 1983. Although 31 state maximums were above $7,000 in 1984, only 9 exceeded $10,000. Thus even among states that have legislated higher maximums there has been a reluctance to go too far beyond the FUT taxable maximum.

Table 1-6
State UI Tax Data, 1960 to 1984

Year	FUT taxable wage base (1)	Ratio of taxable-to-total wages (2)	Average tax rate on taxable wages (percent) (3)	Average tax rate on total wages (percent) (4)	States with tax bases above the FUT tax base[a] (5)
1960	3,000	.611	1.92	1.17	6
1961	3,000	.600	2.05	1.23	6
1962	3,000	.590	2.35	1.39	9
1963	3,000	.581	2.33	1.35	10
1964	3,000	.570	2.24	1.27	15
1965	3,000	.558	2.12	1.18	16
1966	3,000	.553	1.93	1.07	18
1967	3,000	.533	1.66	.89	18
1968	3,000	.517	1.49	.77	22
1969	3,000	.497	1.40	.70	22
1970	3,000	.477	1.37	.65	22
1971	3,000	.453	1.44	.65	23
1972	4,200	.517	1.65	.85	5
1973	4,200	.500	1.96	.98	4
1974	4,200	.475	1.97	.94	5
1975	4,200	.452	1.99	.90	10
1976	4,200	.465	2.50	1.16	20
1977	4,200	.451	2.83	1.27	23
1978	6,000	.496	2.72	1.35	12
1979	6,000	.474	2.72	1.29	14
1980	6,000	.447	2.49	1.11	16
1981	6,000	.423	2.43	1.03	19
1982	6,000	.405	2.53	1.02	24
1983	7,000	.424	2.75	1.17	24
1984	7,000	NA	NA	NA	31

SOURCES: Based on data taken from U.S. Department of Labor, *Unemployment Insurance Financial Data* (1984). Average tax rates in column (3) were computed at The Urban Institute. Data for 1983 are preliminary.

a. This column refers to the 50 states plus the District of Columbia.

NA = not available.

One obvious way to increase the responsiveness of UI taxes to inflation is to index the taxable wage base. Hawaii indexed its wage base in 1965 and several other states followed suit in the mid-1970s. Typically, the tax base is set to a specific percentage, say 67 or 100 percent, of the state's average wage in the previous (calendar or fiscal) year. By 1984 there were 14 states with taxable wage bases indexed to average wages. All nine states with tax bases above $10,000 in 1984 were states where the tax base was indexed. It is clear that indexing has led to larger increases in the tax base than have periodic legislated increases. In chapter 3 we will review the performance of states that have indexed their taxable wage bases to determine if they had less serious trust fund problems in the 1970s and 1980s when compared to the average experience of other states.

Considering the financing difficulties that state UI programs have had since 1970, it seems that stagflation poses especially serious problems. In a period of stagflation total benefit payments increase both because high unemployment raises weeks compensated and because inflation raises average weekly benefits. To the extent that the taxable wage base is fixed in nominal terms, most of the revenue adjustments must take the form of higher employer tax rates. In the aggregate, employer tax rates were not raised sufficiently in the 1970s and in 1980-83 to prevent the need for large scale U.S. Treasury loans. High inflation since 1969 has clearly played a role in the state UI funding problem.

The Costs of Extended Benefits

The Federal-State Extended Benefit (EB) program was enacted in 1970 (PL91-373) to provide up to 13 extra weeks of benefits to exhaustees during recessions. A set of trigger mechanisms was specified that would activate EB payments whenever state and/or national insured unemployment rates exceeded predetermined thresholds.[22] Benefits were first available in 1971, and they have been paid in every year since 1971.

The costs of the EB program are a shared federal-state responsibility with each paying for half of the total. The federal share of EB costs was originally projected to be covered by a .1 percent Federal Unemployment Tax contribution rate in 1970 and 1971 and then a .05 percent rate in later years. To cover the other half of EB costs, states were to tax employers using whatever method they desired. Some states have levied a flat rate tax, while others have experience rated EB costs.

In practice, EB has proven more costly than originally anticipated. Between 1971 and 1976 the federal half of EB costs totaled $3.4 billion while cumulative 1970-76 EB taxes were only about $1 billion.[23] The deficit in the federal share of EB costs was made up by borrowing from the U.S. Treasury. To repay these Treasury advances a "temporary" increase of .2 percent in the FUT tax rate was imposed in 1977 and has been in effect in all subsequent years.[24]

Financing the state share of EB costs has been difficult in several states. The initial federal actuarial cost projections, as reflected in the FUT tax rate increase of 1970, were so low that most states did not change their existing tax schedules. Raising UI tax rates is often controversial and difficult to accomplish, and in many states it was easier to avoid conflicts by retaining existing tax schedules. The impacts of high inflation and the subsequent recessions (with attendent increases in long duration unemployment) meant that a substantial new dollar volume of claims on state trust fund accounts resulted from the EB program.

The state share of EB costs has contributed to the volume of UI loans in the 1970s and 1980s. Employer EB-related contributions are a part of UI taxes in each state and extended benefit payments are debited either to individual employer accounts or to a noncharged benefits account.[25] Large outlays for the state share of EB costs cause state trust funds to be drawn down in exactly the same manner as payments of regular state UI benefits. The cumulative state share of EB costs between 1971 and 1983 was $7.7 billion. Although there are no published estimates on the cumulative amount of state taxes earmarked to pay for EB, they certainly have been much less than the $7.7 billion of benefit payments. Thus, because of EB, deficits in state trust fund accounts between 1971 and 1983 have been larger than they would have been in the absence of this program.

Although EB payments undoubtedly have helped relieve economic hardships among the long term unemployed, it is now clear that the program was created just as state UI was entering a period of heavy demand for benefits. No major new additions to state UI taxes were mandated, and the new federal taxes mandated in 1970 were clearly inadequate to meet the federal share of actual EB costs. As a result EB payments have helped contribute to the UI funding problems recently experienced by several states.[26]

Reviewing the four factors discussed above it does not seem surprising that a state UI funding problem emerged in the 1970s and has been even more severe in 1980-83. High unemployment, uneven regional growth rates, high inflation and unexpected costs of EB all have contributed to the recent tendency for benefit outlays to exceed revenues in state UI. The severity of the funding problem has varied widely from one state to the next. Chapter 2 will examine debtor state experiences and recent adjustments in some detail. Part of chapter 3 will focus on how some states have been able to avoid funding problems. Before descending to the level of individual state experiences, however, it will be useful to briefly review recent developments on the benefit side of state UI programs.

Benefit Payments Since 1970

State UI funding problems could originate from developments in program benefits or revenues or both. Table 1-7 presents national data useful for assessing aggregate benefit payments. Benefit data appear for three long periods (1949-59, 1960-69 and 1970-79) and annually for the years 1970 to 1983. Aggregate benefits as a percentage of total payroll (benefit cost rates), were very similar in the 1950s and 1970s (1.17 and 1.15 percent respectively).[27] Slow growth due to frequent recessions in these decades contributed to a benefit cost rate that was considerably higher than during the 1960s.

Columns 2-5 then focus on four factors that are important in determining benefit payments. Besides the economy's overall unemployment rate, there are three ratios (insured-to-total unemployment, weekly beneficiaries-to-insured unemployment, and weekly benefits-to-average weekly wages) to be considered. Variations in these four factors cause changes in aggregate benefit outlays with increases in any one causing benefit payments to be higher. Growth in the three ratios would suggest that UI programs were becoming more generous either in terms of benefit availability to the unemployed (columns 3 and 4) or the size of weekly benefits (column 5). Column 6 combines the (product of the) three ratios into an overall benefits index.

Unemployment rates have already been discussed. The average rate was higher in the 1970s than in the 1960s and very high in the 1980-83 period. There is a clear positive association between the annual data in columns 1 and 2.

Of the three components in the overall benefits index, the ratio of weekly benefits-to-weekly wages (often referred to as the gross replacement rate) demonstrates a clear upward trend. From the 1950s to the 1970s, the three-decade averages were .335, .346 and .364 respectively. This ratio has

Table 1-7
Measures of State UI Benefit Payments and of Contributing Factors, 1949-1983

Time period	Benefit cost rate[a] (percent) (1)	Total unemployment rate (percent) (2)	Contributing factors			Overall benefit factors index (3) x (4) x (5) (6)
			Ratio of insured-to-total unemployment (3)	Ratio of average weekly beneficiaries-to-insured unemployment (4)	Ratio of average weekly benefit-to-average weekly wage (5)	
1949-59	1.17	4.6	.498	.855	.335	.143
1960-69	1.00	4.8	.426	.854	.346	.126
1970-79	1.15	6.2	.413	.836	.364	.126
1970	1.01	4.9	.441	.840	.357	.132
1971	1.23	5.9	.429	.847	.365	.133
1972	.98	5.6	.379	.843	.361	.115
1973	.79	4.9	.374	.840	.365	.113
1974	1.07	5.6	.439	.833	.365	.133
1975	2.03	8.5	.503	.849	.371	.158
1976	1.39	7.7	.404	.819	.371	.123
1977	1.16	7.1	.380	.823	.364	.114
1978	.93	6.1	.380	.823	.364	.114
1979	.94	5.8	.397	.838	.361	.120
1980	1.34	7.1	.439	.854	.364	.136
1981	1.17	7.6	.368	.859	.359	.113
1982	1.72	9.7	.380	.878	.375	.125
1983	1.43	9.6	.311	.881	.368	.101

SOURCES: Data in columns (1), (4) and (5) taken from U.S. Department of Labor, *Unemployment Insurance Financial Data* (1984). Column (2) is based on the household labor force survey. Column (3) based on UI program data and household labor force data. Column (6) is the product of columns (3), (4) and (5). Data for 1983 are preliminary

a. Benefit outlays as percent of total covered payrolls.

both a trend and a cyclical component. It rises in recessions as more experienced and high wage persons enter the pool of beneficiaries.[28] From column 5 it is clear that weekly benefits in 1980-83 are more generous relative to weekly wages than they were two decades earlier. Note also, however, that this replacement rate was not noticeably higher in 1982-83 than it had been in 1975-76. It may be that the replacement has peaked in the early 1980s.[29]

Insured unemployment includes regular state UI beneficiaries and claimants who are not yet collecting benefits, e.g., those serving a waiting period and some persons whose claims are in dispute. It excludes persons receiving EB, those who have exhausted benefits and persons who do not apply. If waiting periods were becoming shorter, the ratio of weekly beneficiaries-to-insured unemployment would rise. From table 1-7, however, it is clear there is no upward trend in this ratio. If anything, it declined somewhat in the 1970s in comparison to previous decades. This ratio also has a cyclical component so that increases in 1980 and 1982 are normal cyclical occurrences reflecting the increased average duration of claimants in benefit status.

The second obvious trend in the three ratios is the decline in the ratio of insured-to-total unemployment (column 3). Averages for the three decades were .498, .426 and .413 respectively. The downtrend is the result of many influences among which the changing demographic mix of unemployment is undoubtedly the most important. Younger persons and women have come to represent an increasing share of total unemployment. Since they are less likely to collect UI benefits than are adult men, this changing mix has caused the ratio of insured to total unemployment to decline.

This ratio also has a strong cyclical element. In recession, layoffs cause the mix of unemployment to change and job losers become a larger share of total unemployment. Since they are the group most likely to collect benefits, this compositional change raises the ratio of insured-to-total unemployment. Between 1973 and 1975 the ratio increased from .374 to .503 and it also increased between 1979 and 1980.

An interesting research question has arisen regarding the behavior of insured unemployment since 1979. Regression analyses by Burtless (1983) and by Vroman (1984) have shown that insured unemployment has been lower than expected since 1979 and that the gap between insured and total unemployment grew successively larger in each year between 1980 and 1983. Note in table 1-7 that the column 3 ratio fell in 1981 and rose only modestly in 1982 despite the large increase in unemployment of that year. The ratio then fell sharply in 1983 even though the total unemployment rate was virtually unchanged from 1982. Contributing to the recent reductions in insured unemployment have been changes in UI laws and administrative practices as well as the unusually high level of benefit exhaustions since 1979.

Although it seems likely that state UI funding problems have contributed to recent declines in the ratio of insured-to-total unemployment, this has yet to be conclusively demonstrated by careful research. One effect of the recent reductions in this ratio, of course, is to lower total UI benefit outlays in 1980-83.[30] A second element of reduced benefit availability is lower amounts of EB payments since 1981. Because of Reagan Administration changes in EB triggers these payments for long-term joblessness have been much lower, particularly in 1982-83.

The overall benefits index combines movements in the three ratios to produce a summary measure. The index was no higher in 1970-79 than it had been in 1960-69, and both were lower than the average index for the 1950s. The effects of the gradual rise in the replacement rate were more than offset by the decline in the ratio of insured-to-total unemployment. Also note that the overall index was actually lower in 1982 than in 1975, and that the 1983 index is the lowest of any since 1970, more evidence that UI benefits have not been increasing relative to historic norms. Thus the high benefit payout rate observed since 1970 (column 1) has been due to higher unemployment and not to increased availability and generosity of UI benefits.

Summary

The state UI funding problem documented in the first part of this chapter has origins predominantly in high unemployment during 1970-79 and 1980-83, coupled with an insufficiently responsive revenue system. Also contributing to the funding problem have been unusually wide variations in regional growth rates, inflation and increased financial obligations posed by the EB program. Although borrowing has been widespread, even larger deficits would have been incurred in the 1980-83 period if there had not been recent reductions in insured unemployment (and associated regular state UI benefits) and cutbacks in EB payments.

NOTES

1. This amount refers to the debt arising from the payment of regular state UI benefits and the state share (half) of federal-state Extended Benefits or EB. Deficits in the Extended Unemployment Compensation Account (EUCA), a federal UI trust fund account used to pay the federal share of Extended Benefit costs and other temporary long-term benefits provided during 1971-73 and 1975-77, also gave rise to borrowing by this account from the U.S. Treasury. At the end of 1983 the EUCA debt was $6.2 billion making a total debt of $19.5 billion for the entire federal-state system of UI programs. Because the EUCA debt is gradually being repaid by earmarked federal payroll taxes, this component of indebtedness will not be examined in the present report.

2. The federal-state unemployment insurance system was established as the result of the Social Security Act of 1935 (PL 74-271). The Federal Unemployment Tax Act of 1939 (PL 76-379) details the federal payroll tax incorporating federal UI financing provisions that were originally in the Social Security Act. For one description of state UI see chapter 13 in Myers (1981).

3. For one concise description of UI financing provisions for the period from 1935 to 1978, see the Appendix in Mackin (1978). In addition to taxing employers, four states (Alabama, Alaska, New Jersey and Pennsylvania) also levied taxes on covered employees in 1984.

4. If a state maximum tax rate is lower, employers at that maximum receive less than the full offset since that maximum rather than experience determines their rate.

5. One of the federal trust fund accounts is the federal loan fund from which states with depleted reserves may borrow to continue to pay benefits.

6. There are 53 state UI programs in the United States, those in the 50 states plus the District of Columbia, Puerto Rico and the Virgin Islands. The latter two jurisdictions will be excluded from the analysis of the present report.

7. Prior to 1972, federal loans had been made to just three state UI programs. During the 1950s and early 1960s, loans were made to Alaska, Michigan, and Pennsylvania. These loans were fully repaid by the late 1960s.

8. Increments of .3 percent apply strictly in the first two years that FUT penalty taxes are paid by a debtor state. Provisions determining further increments after the second year have changed more than once. In 1984, for example, a debtor state may have a third year penalty tax rate of .6, .7, .8 or .9 percent.

9. Seven different states experienced a .3 percent FUT penalty tax rate for a single year. The states and years were as follows; 1974-Connecticut, 1976-Washington, 1977-Vermont, 1978-District of Columbia and Rhode Island, and 1979-Delaware and Pennsylvania. Penalty taxes are due in January of the year following the year to which they apply.

10. The 12 were Alabama, Arkansas, Florida, Hawaii, Maryland, Michigan, Minnesota, Nevada, New York, Ohio, Oregon and Washington. Massachusetts and Montana completed their debt repayments in 1980.

11. In fact, not one of the four with the largest debts passed comprehensive legislation to improve the fiscal balance in their UI program prior to 1980. New Jersey, which did raise average employer tax rates in 1977-79 and indexed its taxable wages base in 1976, made small voluntary repayments in 1978 and 1979 and Connecticut did so in each year from 1976 to 1979. All of these repayments, however, were made in lieu of FUT penalty taxes and were not truly voluntary repayments.

12. Actual payment of FUT penalty taxes takes place at the end of January in the year following their accrual.

13. The rate applicable has been 10 percent. For one description of these legislative provisions see Hobbie (1982).

14. This legislation also changed the triggering mechanism used to activate EB programs in the states. Subsequent EB payments have been much lower than what would have been paid previously. Because half of EB payments are state financed, this change also helped improve the fiscal balance of UI programs.

15. See Hobbie (1982).

16. The FSC program has no direct financial implications for the states as these long term jobless benefits are financed entirely from federal general revenues. The program was subsequently extended three more times and scheduled to last until the end of March 1985.

17. The 1983 Wisconsin legislative changes that satisfy these TEFRA financial requirements are described in chapter 2.

18. For a state forced to borrow in 1983, the increase in net solvency must be at least 25 percent in 1983 and then 35 and 50 percent in 1984 and 1985. Some states that have made adjustments, e.g., Michigan, made more than a 50 percent net solvency adjustment immediately in 1983. The change in net solvency is computed as the sum of two percentage changes: the increase in taxes and the reduction in benefits where both are measured as changes from a baseline projection based on prior UI laws.

19. To be eligible for lower interest rates in the second and third years of indebtedness, the increases in net solvency needed to be 80 and 90 percent respectively.

20. See Hobbie (1983).

21. See, for example, Perry (1970).

22. Insured unemployment rates (or IURs) are measured as the ratio of insured unemployment to covered employment. The national trigger was eliminated in 1981 and the state trigger thresholds were also revised upward by the 1981 legislation.

23. Data on EB benefit payments are shown in U.S. Department of Labor (1984a). Estimates of annual tax payments by employers for the federal share of EB costs can be made from this same publication.

24. In 1983 a second "temporary" increase in FUT tax rates became effective. The FUT rate was increased by .1 percent to .8 percent of taxable payroll. Part of the increased tax rate was earmarked to pay for the federal share of EB costs.

25. Noncharged benefits are not assigned to individual employer trust fund accounts. They are treated as a common cost to all employers and are financed by flat rate state taxes.

26. Because of changes in the EB triggering mechanism enacted under the Reagan Administration, the EB program will be much smaller in the future. Thus it will not contribute to UI funding problems in future years.

27. Recall from table 1-4 that unemployment rates for men 25 and older were also very similar in the 1950s and 1970s.

28. For one time series analysis of the gross replacement rate see Hight (1980).

29. Until 1979, UI benefits were received as tax-free income. Thus when weekly benefits are considered in relation to after tax weekly wages, the net replacement rate probably rose more rapidly than the gross replacement between the late 1940s and 1978. Hight (1980) has examined both replacement rates. Because UI benefits have been taxable since 1979, this has definitely lowered net replacement rates in recent years.

30. For one analysis of reduced UI benefit payments in the 1980-83 period see Vroman (1984). The paper examines payments under regular state UI programs and extended jobless benefits under the EB and FSC programs.

2
Debtor State Experiences

Underlying the aggregate state UI funding problem are the varied experiences of individual state programs. Some have a longer history of borrowing and debt than others which first needed large loans in 1982. Certain states that borrowed in the 1970s have been debt free in the 1980s while others required additional loans. The present chapter focuses on 10 states whose debts were the largest at the end of 1983. Their combined indebtedness totaled $12.2 billion or 92 percent of the national total. Thus, the state UI funding problem is most acute in these particular jurisdictions.

This chapter has two main objectives: to provide background information on individual state funding problems and to describe the recent legislation enacted to improve the balance between program revenues and outlays. Following a narrative description of individual state experiences, there is a cross-state comparison of debtor state responses. Summary observations are then given at the end of the chapter.

Developments in 10 Debtor States

Table 2-1 identifies 10 states with the largest UI trust fund debts at the end of 1983, listing them according to the total amount of debt (column 5). Measured both by the size of their 1980-83 loans and their 1983 indebtedness, it is obvious that four states have especially large financial problems:

Table 2-1
Ten States with Largest UI Trust Fund Debts at the End of 1983 and Selected Data

State[a]	Net reserve ratio multiple January 1, 1980 (1)	Debt on January 1, 1980 ($ millions) (2)	Average unemployment rate 1980-83 (percent) (3)	Loans 1980-83 ($ millions) (4)	December 31, 1983 debt ($ millions) (5)	December 31, 1983 debt/1982 covered payrolls (percent) (6)
Pennsylvania	b	1,222	9.7	2,587	2,617	4.6
Illinois	b	946	9.9	2,542	2,423	3.7
Michigan	.07	0	13.6	3,047	2,322	5.0
Ohio	.42	0	10.7	2,308	1,976	3.6
Texas	.66	0	6.4	804	685	.8
Wisconsin	1.06	0	9.0	802	626	2.3
Louisiana	.77	0	9.3	529	476	2.2
New Jersey	b	652	7.8	79	422	1.0
Minnesota	.22	0	6.8	548	352	1.7
West Virginia	.21	0	13.0	297	288	3.7
U.S. Total	.41	3,728	8.5	14,903	13,279	1.1

SOURCES: Columns (1), (2) and (5) based on U.S. Department of Labor, *Unemployment Insurance Financial Data* (1984). Columns (3) and (4) based on unpublished data from the U.S. Labor Department. Column (6) computed as the ratio of column (5) to data on total payrolls appearing in *Unemployment Insurance Financial Data*. Only the ten states with the largest debts are shown.

a. Arrayed by size of year-end 1983 debt.

b. Not shown because the net trust fund balance was negative on January 1, 1980.

Pennsylvania, Illinois, Michigan and Ohio. A very similar indication of serious debt problems emerges when debts are measured relative to covered payrolls (column 6).[1] Of the 21 states with debts at the end of 1983, there were nine where the debt exceeded 1.5 percent of payrolls and five where the debt exceeded 3.5 percent of payrolls. The four states with the largest absolute amounts of debt all have debts larger than 3.5 percent of payrolls, and West Virginia is the fifth state with such a large relative debt. Of the four states with debts between 1.5 and 3.5 percent of payrolls, three are also identified in table 2-1 (Wisconsin, Louisiana and Minnesota but not Rhode Island). Thus eight of the nine states with the largest relative debts are present in table 2-1. By and large, the states with big absolute debts also have large relative debts.

Note in table 2-1 that three of the states (Pennsylvania, Illinois and New Jersey) already had substantial debts at the start of 1980, and that the other seven entered the 1980s with generally low reserve ratio multiples. Of the 10, only Wisconsin had a multiple that exceeded 1.0. This group, in other words, includes neither of the two states (Kansas and Mississippi) with adequate reserves, i.e., with reserve ratio multiples of at least 1.5 in January 1980, and only one (Wisconsin) of the eleven states whose multiples fell between 1.0 and 1.49 on that date (recall table 1-2). Column 3 shows that 7 of the 10 (all but Texas, New Jersey and Minnesota) had higher than average unemployment between 1980 and 1983. With low trust fund reserves and higher than average unemployment, it is hardly surprising that these states accumulated debts. The 10 borrowed $13.6 billion or 91 percent of all loans extended during the 1980-83 period. Thus recent loans as well as trust fund debts are heavily concentrated in the 10 jurisdictions.

The following pages briefly review the salient developments in these 10 states. Accompanying the text for each state is an appendix table that shows important summary data on the state's trust fund balances, loans, benefit payments and taxes. These tables that cover the years 1970 to 1983 provide back-up for statements that appear in the text.

Many debtor states enacted important legislation in late 1982 and early 1983 designed to improve the net solvency of their programs. Projections of increased revenues and reduced benefit outlays for later years made at the time of their legislation were contingent upon assumptions about future economic developments, e.g., state unemployment rates and inflation rates. These assumed conditions were not always realized, as some economic recoveries occurred more rapidly than expected while others (particularly in energy-producing states) lagged behind expectations. Even though the actuarial projections may prove to be in error, they are useful for showing what the states thought would happen following their UI legislation. Therefore, where available, these actuarial projections will be used in the present chapter for describing debtor states' revenue and benefit adjustments. Particular attention will be focused on the years 1983-86 since debtor states have been given strong financial incentives, e.g., interest deferrals, to improve net solvency in these years. The size of the state adjustments will be examined as well as the mix of tax increases and benefit reductions.

Pennsylvania

The Pennsylvania economy experienced a prolonged period of slow economic growth in the years after World War II. Covered employment was 3.10 million in 1948 but only 22 percent higher at 3.78 million in 1979. Over this same period, covered employment in the U.S. grew by 116 percent and, as a consequence, Pennsylvania's share of the total declined from 9.4 to 5.3 percent. Employment in coal mining and basic steel manufacturing have grown slowly and both industries are very important to the state's economy.

Pennsylvania has a long history of using federal loans to assist in UI program financing. As net reserves declined sharply in the late 1950s, loans totaling $112 million were obtained during the three years 1959-61. Although only a small fraction of this borrowing was actually used to pay benefits, net trust fund reserves were very low for several years (less than $100 million at the end of each year from 1959 to 1963) and reached a minimum of $3 million at the end of 1961. Between 1964 and 1968, these federal monies were repaid and trust fund reserves were then accumulated throughout the 1960s. One factor contributing to the loan repayment and reserve buildup was an increase in the tax base from $3,000 in 1963 to $3,600 in 1964. A rough estimate (using historic average tax rates on taxable payroll) suggests this $600 increase in the tax base raised roughly $190 million in extra revenues between 1964 and 1971. The net reserve ratio multiple, however, never reached the recommended 1.5 minimum standard.

Pennsylvania is a high benefit state in compensating unemployed workers. Column 8 of appendix table A1 shows that benefits averaged 1.63 percent of covered payroll during the 1970s while the national average was 1.15 percent of payroll. During these 10 years, the average unemployment in the state was only slightly higher than the national average (6.3 versus 6.2 percent). Two primary indicators of high benefit payouts were a consistently high ratio of insured-to-total unemployment and a high ratio of weekly benefits-to-weekly wages (see columns 10 and 11 of table A1). Throughout most of the 1970s, its maximum average potential benefit duration of 30 weeks was the highest of all state UI programs. In 1972 the weekly benefit maximum was raised substantially (from $60 to $85), indexed to be 60 percent of the state's average weekly wage and dependents' benefits were instituted. This benefit liberalization caused the gross replacement rate (average weekly benefits divided by the average weekly wage) to rise from .361 in 1971 to .424 in 1972 (column 11), and the replacement rate has exceeded .40 in all but one of every subsequent year. This particular benefit liberalization occurred just prior to the major inflationary episode of 1973-74, and was not matched by a corresponding indexation of the taxable wage base.

Although statutory tax rates might be increased rapidly to overcome revenue shortfalls arising from an unresponsive tax base, this did not occur to a sufficient degree in Pennsylvania during the 1970s. The average tax rate on taxable wages exceeded the national average in most years (decade averages were 2.42 percent and 2.11 percent respectively), but this was largely offset by a lower taxable wage proportion, the latter caused by higher than average wage levels in Pennsylvania. As a result, for the decade as a whole, taxes as a percent of total payroll were only slightly higher than the national average: 1.08 percent versus 1.00 percent nationally.

The national recession of the mid-1970s was strongly felt in Pennsylvania. The overall unemployment rate rose from 5.1 percent in 1974, to 8.3 percent in 1975 (rates slightly below the national average in both years). From 1976 through 1983, however, the unemployment rate in Pennsylvania has exceeded the national average in every year with the disparities being especially pronounced in 1982 (10.9 versus 9.7 percent) and 1983 (11.8 versus 9.6 percent). Severe recessions in coal mining and basic steel manufacturing are important causes for the very high unemployment of these two recent years.

High unemployment coupled with insufficiently responsive revenues have combined to produce a major UI financing problem in Pennsylvania. Federal loans have been required in every year since 1975 and the amounts have exceeded $200 million in seven different years. In 1982 and 1983, lending grew to $.8 billion and $1.2 billion respectively. The loan total since 1975 exceeds $3.8 billion and more than $2.6 billion was still outstanding at the end of 1983.

Pennsylvania has been slow in repaying these federal advances. Nothing was repaid prior to 1980 when FUT penalty taxes were first levied (on 1979 taxable payrolls). Over $400 million of penalty taxes were paid between 1980 and 1983. The only voluntary loan repayments occurred in 1982 and 1983 when over $700 million of interest-bearing debt was repaid. Even with these repayments, however, the state's interest-bearing debt exceeded $1.1 billion at the end of 1983.

When asked why state taxes were not raised more sharply following the onset of chronic annual deficits, Pennsylvania officials have noted the mixed signals conveyed by federal legislation of the late 1970s. Although there existed a mechanism for automatically imposing FUT penalty taxes, these were overridden twice by federal legislation. There were discussions of outright forgiveness of debts while cost equalization and reinsurance proposals held out the prospect of partial debt forgiveness for the state. Given the possibility of (partial or total) debt forgiveness, there was a reluctance to enact legislation that would increase costs for state employers.

After the start of the 1980 recession, Pennsylvania did enact legislation that reduced benefits and raised taxes.[2] Important benefit provisions included lowering the statutory benefit-wage replacement rate from .58 to .54, instituting a waiting week (which was compensated after four weeks in benefit status), shortening maximum potential benefit duration for some claimants from 30 to 26 weeks, increasing the base period earnings requirement and imposing a more severe disqualification for refusing suitable work. Major tax changes included raising the taxable wage base (to $6,300 in

1980-81 to $6,600 in 1982), increasing the maximum experience rated tax rate (from 4.0 percent in 1979 to 4.9 percent in 1982 and later years), increasing flat rate taxes on covered employers (from 1.7 percent in 1979 to 1.75 percent in 1980-81 and to a maximum of 1.9 percent in 1982 and later years), and increasing the tax rate on new employers. Also a (partly rebatable) flat rate tax of 1 percent of taxable payroll was imposed starting in 1980. Table A1 shows that average tax rates did rise in 1980.[3] Despite this legislation the state continued to borrow in 1981 and even more in 1982 as the state unemployment rate rose to 10.9 percent.

When new loans began to carry interest charges in 1982, ambiguities about the federal attitude towards state indebtedness were ended. Under the Reagan administration, states were to be fully responsible for all old and new debts. As noted, the 1983 Social Security Amendments gave debtor states a way of reducing and deferring their interest costs. This provided a strong incentive for state legislation and Pennsylvania responded very quickly.

An initial set of UI proposals made by Governor Thornburg's administration in April 1983 was found unacceptable by both labor and management representatives. A tripartite committee (labor, business and "neutrals" with the latter including an academic committee chairman and representatives from state agencies, the legislature and the executive branch) was formed and held negotiating sessions that lasted more than two months before reaching an acceptable legislative proposal.[4]

Legislation enacted in July 1983 included provisions to increase business taxes, to tax employees and to reduce UI benefits. Eight separate provisions of the 1983 legislation and their 1983-86 budgetary effects were as follows.[5] (1) Retroactive compensation for the waiting week (after four weeks of benefits) was ended ($183 million). (2) The maximum duration for regular benefits was reduced from a 26-30 week range to a 16-26 week range ($197 million). (3) The weekly benefit amount was reduced by 5 percent from what would have been paid under the prior law ($247 million). (4) A .1 percent payroll tax on total annual wages and salaries of all covered employees was instituted ($236 million). (5) The taxable wage per employee was raised from $7,000 in 1983 to $8,000 in 1984 and later years ($427 million). (6) Employer tax rates were modified in several ways with the effect of substantially increasing average tax rates. The tax rate computation schedule was revised to explicitly recognize recent experience in paying benefits and the reserve ratio balances of individual employers. A statewide flat tax was imposed for years starting in 1984. The maximum tax to defray noncharged and ineffectively charged benefits was reduced from 1.9 to 1.5 percent. In addition to raising total taxes, these provisions increased the importance of experience rating in determining employer taxes ($833 million). The range of employer tax rates was increased from 4.1 percentage points in 1983 to 7.0 percentage points in 1984 and wider ranges in subsequent years. (7) A 15 percent surcharge was added to employer taxes in 1983 ($155 million). (8) A flat rate interest tax was imposed starting in 1984 ($447 million). From their sheer number, it is clear that the 1983 legislative provisions represent a major change in the state's UI statutes and program solvency.

The combined budgetary impact of all eight provisions (tax increases plus benefit reductions) was estimated to be a $2,712 million increase in program solvency for the four-year period 1983-86. Combining employee benefit reductions ($612 million) with the new employee tax ($236 million) as employee sacrifices, these made up 31.3 percent of the change, while employer tax increases ($1,862 million) accounted for the other 68.7 percent.

Due to its 1983 legislation, Pennsylvania can defer interest payments on outstanding loans, pay a lower interest rate (9 percent) in 1983 and be eligible for reduced FUT penalty taxes after 1983. The combined effects of these three provide substantial savings for Pennsylvania employers. Over the 1983-86 period, the total savings is estimated to be $846 million, $552 million in deferred and reduced interest payments on loans and $294 million in lower FUT penalty taxes.[6] To give a more accurate assessment of increased employer costs in 1983-86 due to the 1983 legislation this $846 million should be netted out against the $1,862 million increase noted above. When this is done the net increase in employer taxes over the 1983-86 period becomes $1,016 million and the employer share of the total sacrifice falls from 68.7 percent to 54.4 percent. From the standpoint of net employer tax increases, the burden sharing with workers comes much closer to a 50-50 split.

Under either a net or gross measure of employer tax burdens, it is clear that higher taxes are in store for Pennsylvania employers for several years. The recent legislation, however, clearly improves the program's net solvency and provides the means for eventually eliminating the state's large UI trust fund debt. Even after the enactment of this legislation the problem of UI debt will be present for several years. Under current actuarial projections the indebtedness that was accumulated over so many past years will not be fully eliminated until 1991. The projections show the total debt declining in every year after 1983, voluntary repayments occurring during 1984-86 and FUT penalty taxes (levied at increasing rates) being paid until 1991. Should another recession occur before 1991, of course, the state will face the prospect of renewed borrowing and a further postponement in achieving debt-free status.

Illinois

Illinois is a major industrial state with important concentrations of employment in the manufacture of basic steel, farm and construction equipment, and electronic equipment. Its UI program borrowed heavily in the 1970s and again in the present decade. Total indebtedness at the end of 1983 was $2,423 million, the second highest total of any state.

Throughout most of its history the UI program in Illinois could be characterized as a low cost benefit program. During the periods 1949-59 and 1960-69, for example, employer UI taxes in Illinois as a percentage of covered payroll, averaged about two-thirds of the national average. Table A2 shows this situation persisted in the first half of the 1970s as well. Benefits as a percent of total payroll (column 8) remained below the national average in 1970-74 as each of three important contributors to low benefit costs was also lower than average. Specifically, the state's overall unemployment rate was relatively low, insured unemployment was a low proportion of total unemployment, and weekly benefits were a low proportion of average weekly wages (columns 9, 10, and 11 respectively).

During 1975-79, Illinois continued to experience below average unemployment but UI benefit costs rose sharply. Partly this was due to a generally higher unemployment rate (6.3 percent in 1975-79 versus 4.4 percent in 1970-74) but also there was a substantial liberalization of benefit availability and benefit levels. The latter were the direct consequence of 1975 legislation that took effect in the second half of the year.[7] Traditionally, UI legislation in Illinois had followed the recommendations of a tripartite (labor, management and public) Employment Security Advisory Board where labor representatives focused mainly on questions of benefits while management representatives were more responsible for financing provisions. Between the early

1960s and 1975, management representatives were not willing to propose any important tax increases. Finally, in 1975 labor changed its tactic by offering a bill in the legislature that had not previously been approved by the Advisory Board. The provisions of the bill called for substantial liberalizations of both benefit duration and benefit levels. After employer representatives realized the package was likely to pass, they tried to add financing provisions to the legislation but were not successful. Thus a bill passed that changed benefits without changing taxes. Many expected this bill to be vetoed by then Governor Walker, but it was signed and became effective on July 1, 1975.

There were three important benefit changes in the 1975 legislation. (1) The range of maximum weekly benefit (including maximum dependents' allowances) was raised from $60-105 to $97-135 starting in July 1975. (2) Maximum potential benefit duration was changed from a 10 to 26 week range to a uniform 26 weeks. This increased maximum potential duration for many unemployed workers. (3) Retroactive compensation of the waiting week (after three weeks of benefits) was instituted. The consequences of these changes are apparent in table A2. Weekly benefits as a proportion of weekly wages rose from .343 in 1974 to .412 in 1976 and have remained above the national average in all subsequent years. Similarly the ratio of insured to total unemployment rose and has also remained above the national average ratio. Due to these statutory changes and to increased unemployment, benefits as a percent of payroll have been consistently higher than average since 1976.

Illinois entered the 1970s with a rather modest UI trust fund balance. Although the balance stood at $500 million at the start of 1970, this represented a reserve ratio multiple of only 1.17. Table A2 shows that the multiple thus fell below 1.0 during 1970 and never returned even to this modest level. Borrowing, which first occurred in 1975, was especially heavy in 1976 ($446 million) and an additional $431 million was borrowed in 1977 and 1978. Thus over the 1975-78 period, a debt of $946 million was accumulated, second in size only to Pennsylvania's debt.

Although average tax rates on taxable wages increased measurably in 1976 and 1977, the increases were not sufficient to match the increased benefit payments. Average statutory tax rates did not rise much after 1977 and there was no important increase in the taxable wage base other than the mandatory 1978 increase to $6,000 under the Federal Unemployment Tax. Although the state's gross trust fund reserve balance did increase during 1978 and 1979, net reserves remained negative because the state did not raise taxes by enough to repay its loans. At the start of 1980, the state's gross reserve balance was $486 million but the $946 million of 1975-78 loans was fully outstanding, leaving a net reserve balance of minus $460 million (column 2 of table A2). In fact Illinois did not make any loan repayments until 1981 when FUT penalty taxes were first paid (on the basis of 1980 taxable payrolls). Hopeful of partial or total debt forgiveness, labor and management representatives were reluctant to initiate repayments until federal policy on the treatment of outstanding federal loans was known with certainty.

After a long period of below average unemployment, the Illinois unemployment rate rose sharply in 1980 to 8.3 percent (1.2 percentage points above the national average) and then again higher to 11.3 percent in 1982. As a consequence the state has experienced benefit payout rates in the 1980s that are higher than in the entire previous history of its program.[8] Having no substantial trust fund balance to draw upon, a small loan of $38 million was needed in 1980 and then loans of $487, $844, and $1,178 million were required in 1981, 1982, and 1983. To reduce interest payments the state repaid over $700 million of interest-bearing loans, mainly during 1983.

Illinois enacted legislation in both 1981 and 1983 to improve the fiscal health of its UI program. Although the 1983 legislation was the more significant of the two, the 1981 bill, a product of recommendations by the Advisory Board, is also worth noting.[9] It ended the retroactive compensation of the waiting week, raised base period monetary eligibility requirements, imposed an emergency flat rate tax surcharge of .4 percent and raised the taxable wage base to $7,000 in 1982. At the time of its passage this bill was expected to reduce the accumulation of new debt over the next few years by more than $400 million.

As 1982 unfolded, it became clear that the UI program continued to have a fiscal imbalance. The total amount of new loans in 1982 was the largest in the entire history of the program. Governor Thompson had previously appointed a Labor-Management Task Force in November 1981 to examine the program and propose a legislative package. During late 1982 the Task Force, whose members included leaders from labor, management, and the state government, assembled for a legislative proposal to substantially raise taxes and reduce benefits. For the 1983-86 period, its proposals were estimated to increase program solvency by about $2 billion. Through internal negotiations, the Task Force agreed that 60 percent of the total change was to be tax increases and 40 percent to be benefit reductions. Their proposals were eventually passed but with a sunset provision. As of July 1, 1986 all changes were to terminate and tax and benefit statutes were to automatically revert to their former status.[10]

The legislative package was passed in mid-April 1983 and took effect on April 24. Although it had been drafted prior to the passage of the 1983 Social Security Amendments, the

Illinois law enabled the state to take advantage of some of the federal law's interest deferral and FUT penalty tax provisions. The state was able to defer 80 percent of interest payments due in 1983 and 1984 (but not in 1985) and to reduce FUT penalty taxes starting in 1983.

Important benefit provisions in the 1983 law were as follows. (1) The replacement rates (benefits as a percentage of base period average weekly wages) were lowered—from 50 to 48 percent for single persons, from 60 to 55 percent for a beneficiary with a dependent spouse and from 66.1 to 62.4 percent for a beneficiary with dependent children. (2) The computation of the base period average weekly wage was changed—from high quarter wages divided by 13 to highest two quarter wages divided by 26. For many claimants this change reduces the average weekly wage used in determining weekly benefits. (3) The automatic indexing of the maximum weekly benefit to the state average weekly wage was suspended between April 1983 and June 1986. Predetermined maximum weekly benefit amounts were assigned for this period. Thus, for a new beneficiary with no dependents, the previous maximum of $168 was reduced to $154 between April 1983 and January 1984 and then to $161 between February 1984 and June 1986. The effect of these three changes on weekly benefits is already apparent. Average weekly benefits fell from $151.15 in the final three months of 1982 to $136.04 (or by 10 percent) in the final three months of 1983.

There were also major changes in several tax provisions. (4) The taxable wage base was raised to $8,000 between April 1983 and December 1984 and then to $8,500 for the following 18 months. (5) The maximum experience rated employer tax rate was increased from 5.3 percent in 1983 to the following ranges: 5.5-6.3 percent in 1984, 6.4-6.6 percent in 1985 and 6.5-6.7 percent in 1986.[11] (6) An adjusted state experience factor was added to the 1983-1986 tax rate schedule.

In 1983 the factor was 21 percent, meaning that experience rated tax rates were multiplied by 1.21 in arriving at the final tax rate. It is expected that similar sized state experience factors will also apply in each of the years 1984-86. (7) The flat rate emergency surcharge in effect since 1982 at a rate of .4 percent was raised temporarily to .6 percent for the first half of 1986. (8) The taxation of local government units was changed from a flat 1 percent rate (irrespective of experience) to an experience rated arrangement like that applied to private sector employers.[12] The combined effects of these tax changes was both to increase average employer tax rates and to increase the effective degree of experience rating.

The 1983 Illinois law will bring about a major change in the program's actuarial balance. The total change in program solvency during 1983-86 is estimated to be $1,940 million with benefit cutbacks of $780 million (40 percent) and tax increases of $1,160 million (60 percent). We were not able to secure actuarial data showing the budgetary impacts of individual provisions, merely the totals for the tax and benefit changes.[13]

It should be noted that the $1,160 million of employer tax increases refer just to gross tax increases from this legislation. It is estimated that the 1983 legislation will save Illinois employers $530 million between 1983 and 1986 in the form of deferred interest payments ($389 million) and lower FUT penalty taxes ($141 million).[14] When these savings are considered, the net tax increase becomes $630 million and the employer share of the net change in program solvency becomes 44.7 percent.

Clearly the 1983 legislation will bring about a major improvement in the solvency of the Illinois UI program. It does a great deal to offset the fiscal imbalance created by the 1975 legislation. At the time of its enactment it was estimated that the state's borrowing needs during 1983-86 would be reduced from $2.9-3.0 billion to $.9 billion. Since it has a July 1986 sunset provision, however, it also seems clear that Illinois will need to reexamine its program's solvency again in 1985 or 1986. When the legislation expires in mid-1986, the state's debt may still be between $600 million and $1,000 million.

Michigan

Because so much automobile production occurs in this single state, the health of the Michigan economy is closely tied to the fortunes of the U.S. automobile industry. Demand for autos is extremely volatile and changes in production show up immediately in state economic indicators. Since late 1979, demand for domestic autos has been uncharacteristically low for a very long period. This is reflected in the state's very high unemployment rate and in its UI trust fund difficulties. Between 1980 and 1983 Michigan borrowed $3.0 billion, more than any other state in these years.

Michigan is one of three states whose UI program received loans prior to 1972. Three years of low auto demand in the mid-1950s (1954, 1956, and 1958) caused its trust fund to be sharply reduced and $113 million was borrowed in 1958. Although this loan was never actually used to pay UI benefits, the state's net reserves fell below $100 million at the end of 1958 and 1959 and again in 1961 and 1962. The 1958 loan was paid off between 1963 and 1968 and net trust fund reserves were also accumulated. Net reserves were $630 million at the start of 1970 but the reserves ratio multiple was only .85 (see columns 1 and 2 of table A3). Thus Michigan entered the 1970s with a net reserve balance slightly more than half of the suggested ICESA minimum standard.

Michigan has higher than average UI benefit costs. During the 1970s, benefits as a percent of covered payroll averaged 1.41 percent compared to a national average of 1.15 percent. Table A3 shows that two factors in the high rate of benefit payouts are high unemployment rates and a higher than average ratio of insured unemployment to total unemployment. Michigan's unemployment rate exceeded the national average in every year from 1970 to 1983 and the difference averaged 1.7 percentage points (7.9 versus 6.2 percent) in the 1970s. The high ratio of insured to total unemployment reflects several factors. These include the large share of state unemployment in manufacturing, usually more likely to be insured than other unemployment, and eligibility requirements that tended to be less stringent than they were elsewhere in that period.

Although Michigan is a high wage state, its UI benefit levels had been quite modest. In 1979, the weekly benefit maximum was $97 for a single person (up to $136 with dependents' allowances) and the average replacement rate for weekly benefits (column 11 of table A3) was below the national average. Starting in 1981, benefit levels were sharply increased as a result of UI legislation (to be described below). Prior to that time, however, the high rate of benefit payments reflected high unemployment and a high proportion of the unemployed receiving compensation but not a high level of weekly benefits.

Employer taxes have also tended to be higher than the national average in Michigan. Tax rates on taxable wages averaged nearly 3 percent in the 1970s compared to a national average of 2.11 percent. Because it is a very high wage state and because its tax base has not exceeded the FUT tax base systematically by large amounts, the ratio of taxable to total wages in Michigan is much lower than average. This low ratio offsets much of the effect of high average statutory rates. Thus, the state's average tax rate on total wages during the 1970s was 1.22 percent compared to the national average of 1.00 percent.

When unemployment rose to 12.5 percent in 1975, Michigan's modest UI trust fund balance was quickly depleted. Loans in 1975 and 1976 totaled $571 million and represented 37 percent of combined payouts for regular benefits and for EB. Statutory tax rates and the taxable wage base were then increased by enough in the 1976-79 period to pay off the federal loans. However, the trust fund balance at the start of 1980 was only $112 million and the reserve ratio multiple was a scant .07. When unemployment rose in the 1980s there was no outstanding debt, but neither was there a sizeable trust fund cushion to help defray large increases in benefit payouts.

Payouts rose sharply in 1980 as the state's unemployment rate moved upward to 12.4 percent, just .1 percent below its previous peak reached in the trough recession year 1975. Unemployment remained high in 1981 and then increased to 15.5 percent and 14.2 percent in 1982 and 1983 respectively. Over these four years, total benefit payments from Michigan's UI trust fund were $5.2 billion and employer taxes only covered about half of this total. To meet this unusual demand for benefits, the state borrowed about $3.0 billion in four years and $2.3 billion remained outstanding at the end of 1983. Of the $724 million in loan repayments made during 1982 and 1983, all but $40 million were voluntary payments to reduce the interest bearing debt. As 1983 ended, this component of the total debt equaled $800 million.

Michigan has enacted two major UI laws in the 1980s. The first bill passed in late 1980 had three main provisions that took effect on March 1, 1981.[15] (1) The qualifying requirement for monetary eligibility was increased from 14 to 18 weeks of work in the base period and the minimum weekly earnings was raised from $25.01 to 20 times the minimum wage (or to $67.00 in 1981). (2) The disqualification period for a voluntary quit without good cause was changed from a 13-week benefit suspension to a suspension for the duration of unemployment. (3) Weekly benefits were increased substantially and the basis for computing benefits was modified. The previous benefit formula replaced 60 percent of gross weekly wages subject to a maximum that ranged from $97 to $136 (the maximum for a claimant with four or more dependents). The new formula replaced 70 percent of after-tax (or net) weekly wages up to a maximum of 58 percent of the state's average weekly wage (or $182 in 1981). This benefit liberalization is clearly reflected in published data on weekly benefits that increased from $101.87 in 1980 to $154.38 in 1982 and gross replacement rates (column 11 in table A3) which rose from .316 in 1980 to .416 in 1982. The change in weekly benefits was the largest for any two-year period in the history of Michigan's UI program.

Enactment of a substantial benefit liberalization in a year when the state's UI program had to borrow $842 million is a monumental example of poor timing that also shows the influence of labor union legislative strength. Weekly benefit maximums in Michigan had been frozen at the $97-$136 range since 1975, and labor representatives felt it appropriate to raise and index maximum benefits. Although it could be argued that an increase in weekly benefits was desirable, the extent of the increase was excessive. Two factors aided in the passage of this bill: optimism about the future course of state unemployment and strong employer opposition to the previous treatment of voluntary quits. Employer groups believed that benefits paid to voluntary quitters represented a major abuse in the UI program and that as much as $200 million was being spent annually to compensate quitters. By trading the revised, i.e., toughened, treatment of quits along with higher qualifying requirements for the weekly benefit liberalization, labor representatives were able to build a coalition to pass the 1980 bill.

Cost estimates underlying the 1980 bill suggested that perhaps as much as half of the extra payouts arising from higher weekly benefits would be recouped by the changes in monetary eligibility and the voluntary quit disqualification.[16] This might have been true if unemployment had declined. Because unemployment remained high in 1981 and then increased again in 1982, subsequent benefit outlays greatly exceeded those expected at the end of 1980. A rough calculation suggests that 1981 and 1982 outlays were $217 and $577 million higher as a result of the increases in weekly benefits.[17]

As the economic downturn of 1981-82 progressed, it became obvious that Michigan's UI debt was destined to keep growing. In 1982 alone, the state borrowed $1,184 million and $694 million was interest-bearing debt. Early in 1982 a Working Group of employer representatives was appointed by the director of the State Department of Commerce. The Group was asked to study the state's UI financing system and to develop policy recommendations. One outgrowth of the Working Group's efforts was a careful and systematic description of Michigan's current and likely future debt situation if no steps were taken.[18] Under its current law the state debt was projected to grow to $3.8 billion by the end of 1986. Major increases in interest costs and FUT penalty taxes were clearly in store starting in 1983.

Later in 1982 a set of legislative recommendations was forwarded to Governor Milliken and a legislative package was proposed in September. Several of the original provisions were modified or dropped altogether, e.g., a payroll tax on covered employees, in subsequent legislative developments. Eventually, however, a major UI bill was assembled and enacted in December 1982. At the time of its passage the bill was projected to increase taxes and reduce benefits by about $3.6 billion over the four years 1983-86.[19] One of the tax provisions was to raise the tax base to $8,000 in 1983 and to higher levels in 1984-86. Since 1982, federal legislation (TEFRA) raised the FUT tax base from $6,000 in 1982 to $7,000 in 1983, only the increments of Michigan's tax base above $7,000 should be counted in estimating the effects of the December 1982 law. After this correction is made, the estimate of the total increase in program solvency becomes $3.1 billion,[20] still a major change in benefits and taxes.

Four major changes in benefits and their 1983-86 budgetary impacts were as follows. (1) The weekly benefit maximum was frozen during 1983-86 at its 1982 level of $197 ($601 million). (2) The replacement rate was reduced from .70 to .65 of after-tax weekly wages ($257 million). (3) The base period weeks of work requirement was raised from 18 to 20 weeks ($150 million). (4) The weekly wage used to qualify as a week of work in the base period was raised from 20 to 30 times the minimum wage, i.e., from $67 in 1982 to $100 in 1983 ($84 million). Benefit reductions under these four provisions totaled $1,092 million.

There were six main tax provisions. (5) The taxable wage base was raised to $8,000 in 1983 and by $500 increments for the next three years ($724 million). (6) The maximum annual percentage point increment allowed in the tax rate on an employer already at a rate of 5.0 percent or higher was increased from .5 to 1.0 in 1983, to 1.5 in 1984, to 2.0 in 1985 and totally eliminated in 1986 ($168 million). (7) The component of the state tax schedule designed to hasten the accumulation of balances by low and negative balance employers was modified. This so-called Account Building Component (or ABC) had its replenishment proportions and maximum rate increased so that deficient balances would be eliminated more quickly ($417 million). (8) Starting in 1984 the state share of extended benefits was to be experience rated ($250 million). (9) The partial tax credit allowed against the flat-rate Nonchargable Benefit Component (or NBC) of the state UI tax for payment of FUT penalty taxes was eliminated for negative balance employers ($88 million). (10) A special solvency tax for negative balance employers was instituted to finance interest charges on the debt with maximum rates of .5 percent in 1983, 1.0 percent in 1984 and 2.0 percent in later years ($347 million). These tax changes raised substantial new revenues ($1,994 million in 1983-86) and increased the effective degree to which Michigan employers were experience rated.

The 1982 Michigan tax changes were especially notable for the way they concentrated increased tax burdens on negative balance employers. The maximum UI tax rate of 10 percent, plus a solvency tax for interest that could rise to 2.0 percent, could apply in 1986 while the minimum rate could be as low as 1 percent. This combined with an increased flexibility of year-to-year tax rate changes will produce a revenue structure that is more responsive to trust fund balances than in earlier years.

As noted, the Michigan legislation will cause a major improvement in program solvency over the 1983-86 period. Gross employer tax increases of $1,994 million coupled with benefit reductions of $1,092 million were estimated to increase program solvency by $3,086 million in these four years. Of the gross changes, employer tax increases account for 64.6 percent of the total while benefit reductions account for the remaining 35.6 percent.

Subsequent to its passage the 1982 Michigan law was found to satisfy the conditions for interest deferrals and FUT penalty tax relief given in the Social Security Amendments of 1983.[21] The state qualifies for deferral of 80 percent of its 1983-85 interest payments, lower interest rates on its 1983-85 loan balances and a partial cap on its FUT penalty tax rate. Combined, these elements of financial relief will save Michigan employers $606 million over the 1983-86 period.[22] Thus, the net increase in employer taxes is $1,388 million, i.e., the $1,994 million less $606 million. When these tax savings are recognized, the employer share of the net change in program solvency becomes 56.0 percent. Under either measure of employer-employee burden sharing, the state has made a major improvement in UI program solvency. Even with this improvement, however, the state will probably have a debt of at least $500 million at the end of 1986.

Ohio

Ohio is another large industrial state that has experienced a major UI funding problem in the 1980s. The state economy is dependent upon basic steel and auto manufacturing. Both industries have suffered from low demand between 1980 and 1983 and this underlies the state's recent UI trust fund problems. Borrowing that has exceeded $200 million in each year since 1980 was especially large in 1982 and 1983.

Ohio has traditionally had a low cost/low benefit UI program. Average employer tax rates and benefit cost rates were roughly three-quarters of their respective national averages in the 1970s (see columns 8 and 12 in table A4). Because it depends on cyclical durable goods industries, the state has a history of volatile unemployment rates. Ohio's unemployment rate exceeded the national average in trough years like 1970, 1971, and 1975, but for the 1970s as a whole, unemployment in the state was roughly equal to the national average. Lower than average benefit costs have traditionally been the result of two factors; a lower than average proportion of the unemployed are compensated and weekly benefits have replaced a low percentage of worker wages (columns 10 and 11 in table A4). Major changes in the computation of weekly benefits were enacted in the mid-1970s. Between 1973 and 1974, the weekly benefit maximum for a single claimant was raised from $60 to $77 and in 1975 the maximum was indexed to the state's average weekly wage. Since that time, the state's benefit replacement rate has consistently exceeded the national average.

Throughout the history of its UI program employer tax rates have been quite low. This has been accomplished by having low statutory tax rates on taxable wages and by keeping the tax base equal to the base for the Federal Unemployment Tax (FUT). During the 1970s, Ohio's average tax rate on taxable wages exceeded the national average only in 1977 (column 15 of table A4). Because it is a high wage state that has always used the FUT taxable maximum, taxable wages as a percent of total payroll have been lower than the national average in all years.

Ohio's reserve ratio multiple at the start of 1970 (column 1) was below 1.5 but remained near 1.0 until 1975 when the recession substantially depleted its trust fund. The reserve ratio multiple has not been as high as .5 in any year since 1975. A very small federal loan ($2 million) was obtained in 1977 but repaid in the same year. Although average tax rates were raised substantially in 1977 and 1978 (to 2.84 and 2.71 percent respectively) they were then permitted to decline in 1979 and 1980 even though the state's trust fund had not yet been rebuilt to an adequate level.

When unemployment increased sharply in 1980, the comparatively small trust fund balance of $513 million was quickly depleted and loans of $246 million and $354 million were needed in 1980 and 1981. A further sharp rise in unemployment in 1982 to 12.5 percent led to loans of $1,136 million and $574 million in the next two years. Many of these loans were interest-bearing and, despite repaying $275 million of interest-bearing loans in 1982 and 1983, interest-bearing debt at the end of 1983 stood at $1,040 million. Thus, although a sizable debt was only recently acquired, much of the debt carries interest charges that require financing through some form of tax increase.

As events of 1982 unfolded, it was clear that legislation was needed to restore fiscal balance in the state's UI program. Interest groups representing labor and management, however, were both adamant that their own constituents not shoulder most of the adjustment costs. There also was a reluctance to recognize the full extent of the fiscal imbalance, hence the scale of the required legislative remedy.

In late 1982 a UI bill based largely on ideas of the state's seven-person Unemployment Compensation Advisory Council was introduced into the Ohio legislature. This bill was passed in December 1982. It changed both taxes and benefits for 1983 but had a sunset provision cancelling all changes as of January 1, 1984. Although it was obvious to many that Ohio's UI financial imbalance was a much more serious long-run problem, the sunset provision was included to satisfy concerns about overreacting to the current deficit. Many Ohio employer representatives felt a strong economic upturn was in the offing and that the upturn would substantially reduce the need for a long term legislative remedy.

After the 1983 Social Security Amendments were enacted, Ohio legislators could see the financial advantages of legislation covering a longer time period. In June 1983, a second UI bill was passed whose provisions covered 1984 and 1985. This built upon and extended many provisions of the 1982 bill. It also had a sunset clause to restore benefits and taxes to pre-1983 schedules after its expiration in 1985.[23] These two bills made Ohio eligible for interest deferrals in 1983-85, a lower interest rate in 1983 and lower FUT penalty tax rates after 1983. The total 1983-85 change in program solvency was $1,339 million.[24]

Important provisions of the Ohio legislation and 1983-85 budgetary impacts were as follows. (1) The maximum weekly benefit amounts were frozen at their 1982 levels for the succeeding three years, i.e., $147 for a single person and up to $233 including dependents' allowances ($213 million). (2) Compensation for the waiting period after three weeks in benefit status was ended ($106 million). (3) The level of weekly earnings required to be counted as a base period week of employment toward satisfying the qualifying requirement was raised from $20.00 to $85.10 ($17 million). (4) The computation of the weekly benefit amount was modified so as to be rounded down, instead of rounded up, to whole dollars ($13 million). The total of all benefit reductions was $351 million.

Four major tax changes were also legislated. (5) The tax base per employee was raised to $8,000 in 1984 and 1985 ($304 million). (6) The range of experience rated tax rates was expanded from .1-3.8 percent in 1982 to .2-5.1 percent in 1983-84 and to .2-5.4 percent in 1985 ($342 million). (7) The mutualized flat rate tax applied to all covered employers was increased from .5 percent in 1982 to .6 percent in 1983-85 ($68 million). (8) The minimum safe level tax rate (a statewide flat rate tax to increase the state's account balance) was raised from .5 percent in 1982-83 to 1.0 percent in 1984-85 ($270 million). Combined tax increases were projected to raise revenues by $988 million in 1983-85.[25]

As in the other three states with very large debts the Ohio legislation included several major changes in both the revenues and benefit sides of its UI program. Of the $1,339 million change in program solvency, $988 million or about three-fourths of the total took the form of employer tax increases. Because the Ohio laws qualified the state for interest deferrals, lower interest charges and lower FUT penalty taxes, the gross employer tax increases are partly offset by reduced interest costs and lower FUT penalty taxes. It is estimated that these savings in 1983-85 are $456 million ($411 million in interest payments and $45 million in penalty taxes).[26] Thus the legislation represents a net increase of $532 million in employer taxes for the three years. Of the total $883 million net change in program solvency ($1,339 million less $456 million) the employer share is computed to be .602 or three-fifths.

As a result of the 1982 and 1983 legislation Ohio debt at the end of 1985 is projected to be considerably smaller than it otherwise would have been. At the time of its passage, the 1983 bill was projected to reduce the debt from $3,568 million to $2,274 million at the end of 1985.[27] Because actual benefit outlays in 1983 and 1984 have declined by more than anticipated, the debt has declined more rapidly than expected. Thus, in the short run the debt has been reduced but by no means eliminated. It is likely the debt will be between $600 million and $1,000 million at the end of 1985. Since the provisions of the 1983 legislation will expire at that time it seems likely that additional legislation will be required to eliminate the remaining debt.

Texas

The Texas economy has experienced rapid and sustained economic growth since World War II. As a major repository of petroleum reserves and as the largest oil producing state, it benefited from the sharp oil price increases of 1973-74 and 1979-80. The state has also been successful in encouraging the growth of defense-related production and many other manufacturing activities. Texas, which grew especially rapidly in the the 1970s, now has the third largest state economy, ranking behind only California and New York.

Two growth indicators available from UI program data clearly illustrate the long-run prosperity of the Texas economy. Total covered employment increased from 1.19 million in 1948 to 2.57 million in 1969 and then to 5.21 million in 1982. Respectively, the Texas share of national employment was 3.6, 4.9, and 7.4 percent for these three years. For the same three years the Texas average weekly wage in covered employment grew from 77.0 to 93.3 and then to 105.2 percent of the U.S. average weekly wage. Thus both the employment share and relative wages in Texas have grown markedly since 1948.

Traditionally the Texas UI program has paid low benefits and imposed very low tax rates on covered employers. For the periods 1949-59 and 1960-69 employer taxes averaged .44 and .46 percent of covered payroll. With the state's boom economy of the 1970s, the average tax rate was even lower, averaging only .27 percent of covered wages for the years 1970-79. Despite its long-run prosperity, Texas exhausted its trust fund reserves in 1982 and required federal UI loans in 1982, 1983, and 1984.

Table A5 displays summary data on UI benefits, taxes and trust fund balances for the years 1970-83. Benefits as a percent of payroll during the 1970s averaged .34 percent in Texas compared to a national average of 1.15 percent. Three reasons for low benefits were: (i) lower than average unemployment, (ii) a low ratio of insured to total unemployment and (iii) a low ratio of weekly benefits to average weekly wages (columns 9, 10 and 11). For the 14 years covered by table A5, each of the three benefit indicators was below the national average in every year with only two exceptions (the ratio of weekly benefits-to-weekly wages in 1982 and 1983). The ratio of insured-to-total unemployment in Texas has typically been less than half of the U.S. average. The only indicators showing a benefit liberalization is the weekly benefit/weekly wage ratio. Since 1977 Texas has indexed its maximum weekly benefit to increase by $7 for each $10 increase in manufacturing average weekly wages. As a result, the maximum benefit rose from $63 in 1977 to $168 in 1983 or from .298 to .480 of the state's average weekly wage. The replacement rates shown in column 11 of table A5 reflect these increases in the maximum since 1977.

Texas has long been noted for its low employer tax rates. Its tax base per worker has never exceeded the tax base for the Federal Unemployment Tax. Its statutory rates on taxable wages have typically been one-quarter of the national average. The combination of low tax rates and a low tax base has meant that effective tax rates are unusually low. In many years taxes as a percent of payroll have been lower in Texas than in any other state UI program.

Texas entered the 1970s with a reserve ratio multiple of 2.19. This dipped below 1.5 during 1973 and then below 1.0 in 1975. Note in table A5 that the reserve ratio multiple (column 1) was never rebuilt to 1.0 (much less to 1.5) despite the continued prosperity and low unemployment of the late 1970s. In the 1980s, the Texas unemployment rate has remained well below the national average but it did increase to 6.9 percent in 1982 and then to 8.0 percent in 1983. The 1980-83 recession finally affected the energy producing industries in 1982 and this is responsible for much of the recent increase in Texas unemployment.

Because its start of year trust fund balance was very low in 1982, the increased benefit payouts exhausted the trust fund and loans of $143 million were required late in the year. Then as unemployment rose in 1983 an added $661 million was borrowed. All of the Texas debt, $685 million at the end of 1983, is interest-bearing. The size of the debt, however, is much smaller than in the four largest debtor states. Expressed as a percentage of 1982 total state payrolls, for example, the 1983 Texas debt is .8 percent whereas the 1983 debt in Ohio is 3.6 percent of its payrolls (column 6 in table 2-1).

Early in 1982 it became apparent that Texas would soon exhaust its net reserves and need additional funds to keep paying benefits. Although general revenues could have been used for this purpose, it was decided in a special three-day September legislative session to borrow from the federal UI loan fund (like other debtor UI programs) and then repay the loans in 1983 and 1984.[28] At the time of the 1982 legislation it was anticipated that the state would need to borrow about $250 million through May 1983. The September 1982 bill had tax provisions to finance the interest payments on anticipated borrowings (flat rate taxes on taxable payroll of .3 percent in 1982 fourth quarter and .1 percent in 1983 first quarter) as well as surtaxes to pay off the loans and rebuild the trust fund. The latter were to be levied at rates of .3 percent in 1983, no higher than .5 percent in 1984 and possibly higher rates in 1985. Anticipated surtax rates for 1984 and 1985 were .5 and .3 percent respectively. For employers with tax rates above the state minimum there were small additional surtax levies that ranged from .05 percent to .25 percent.

A major motivation for the September 1982 legislation was the desire to avoid even larger tax increases in 1983. Under the prior statute a special surtax was levied on employers at a rate of .1 percent for each $5 million that the trust fund fell below a $225 million floor (as of the previous October 1). Since the balance on October 1, 1982 was only $77 million, the prospective 1983 surtax rate was 3.0 percent of taxable payrolls. This flat rate assessment, about six times the 1982 average tax rate, would have increased tax revenues by roughly $1 billion. To avoid such a sharp increase in employer taxes, the surtax rate schedule was revised. The new schedule added .1 percent for each $45 million that the trust fund was below the $225 million floor. Application of the new schedule in 1983 resulted in a surtax rate of .3 percent rather than 3.0 percent.

Under economic projections made in the fall of 1982, it was anticipated that the Texas trust fund balance would remain negative throughout 1983, but then become positive in mid-1984 and exceed $200 million by mid-1985. At that time it appeared that the 1982 legislation accomplished three things: prevented a sharp tax increase in 1983, provided funding for interest payments on federal loans and enhanced revenues by enough to gradually rebuild the trust fund balance. Compared to what would have been raised by a perpetuation of prior tax rates, the 1982 legislation was expected to increase 1983-85 revenues by more than $550 million.

The Texas economy did not experience the anticipated recovery in 1983, but rather continued to decline and the unemployment rate increased above 1982 levels. By early 1983 it appeared the state might have to borrow as much as $1 billion rather than the $250 million expected in the previous September. In late January 1983, the Governor's Task Force on Emergency Jobs and the Unemployment Trust Fund was created. An eight-member committee was charged "to develop a plan . . . to set the Unemployment Compensation Trust Fund on a course of long-term solvency."[29] Task Force recommendations made in April were the basis for a legislative package that was enacted in late May.

The May 1983 legislation provided for substantially increased tax revenues between 1983 and 1986.[30] It also prevented yet another sharp notch in future employer surtaxes. The maximum surtax for 1984 was .5 percent but projections suggested the October 1984 trust fund debt would be nearly $1 billion. Under the revised surtax schedule (.1 percent for each $45 million below a $225 million floor) the 1985 surtax rate could have been 2.5 percent. Ironically, it was precisely this type of sharp tax increase that the 1982 legislation was designed to avoid. As in 1982, then, the 1983 legislation caused future tax rates to increase but by less than what the previous law would have required. This is a second example of a statute that raised tax revenues but by less than its predecessor. Between 1983 and 1986 state taxes will be increased by over $1 billion (compared to a continuation of 1982 tax rates) and there will also be FUT penalty taxes. As with the 1982 legislation, all of the 1983 solvency adjustments were made in taxes with no changes in UI benefits.

The main tax provisions and estimated 1983-86 revenue effects were as follows.[31] (1) There were increased taxes to pay for interest charges on the higher loan amounts. A surcharge equal to 5 percent of 1982 taxes was levied in the second quarter of 1983 ($34 million). Surtaxes equal to 25 and 10 percent respectively of previous year taxes were due in 1984 and 1985 ($166 million). A flat rate tax of .1 percent was to be levied in 1986 ($31 million). The total of new interest taxes was $231 million. (2) Loan repayment taxes of .1 percent were imposed for eight consecutive calendar quarters starting in the third quarter of 1983 ($400 million). (3) The basis for levying taxes to rebuild the state's trust fund was changed. In the future, the floor and ceiling on the October 1 trust fund balance were to be respectively 1 and 2 percent of taxable wages. When the actual balance fell below the floor, experience rated taxes with potential annual rate changes of up to 2 percent of taxable payroll were to be imposed.This replaced the previous schedule of a flat .1 percent for each $45 million that the balance fell short of the floor. (No estimate is available for the effect of this change on 1983-86 revenues.) (4) The basis for financing benefit payments that cannot be assigned to the individual accounts of active employers (noncharged benefits, ineffectively charged benefits and uncollectable charges) was changed. Previously the replenishment tax that covered these charges had been levied as a proportionate surtax added to each employer's basic UI taxes. In future years the replenishment tax will be levied half as a proportionate surtax and half as a flat rate tax with rates of .34, .23 and .20 percent in 1984, 1985 and 1986 respectively. This change which is projected to leave total replenishment tax revenues unchanged effectively shifts more of this tax burden to employers with low UI tax rates.

The increased revenues under the 1983 law will not be sufficient to repay all loans by the end of 1984. Therefore Texas employers are faced with the prospect of FUT penalty taxes with rates of .3 percent in 1985 and .6 percent in 1986. The total revenue to be raised from these taxes will be about $450 million. Texans anticipate their debt will be totally repaid during 1986. Current projections suggest that the trust fund balance will reach $500 million by the end of 1986.

The recent deficits and borrowing in Texas illustrate that even a very robust state economy can develop a UI financing problem if taxes are kept low and trust fund reserve ratios are allowed to shrink. The scale of the state's financing problem is small compared to that of the four large debtor states. State tax increases arising from 1982 and 1983 legislation coupled with FUT penalty taxes will eliminate the debt by the end of 1986. Part of the state's motivation to repay the debt promptly is the interest that now accrues on outstanding debts. One positive consequence of the 1982 and 1983 legislation is that Texas now has a much better procedure for making annual tax rate adjustments, i.e., one that produces smoother rate adjustments, in response to fluctuations in trust fund balances. The minimum and maximum fund balances are indexed to taxable wages, and tax rates change automatically when balances fall outside the proscribed 1 to 2 percentage point range. Some years of experience with the current tax adjustment mechanism will be needed before full confidence can be placed in it. Also, since it has such low UI benefits (as a percent of total payroll) it seems sensible that recent adjustments to improve program solvency should take the form of tax increases. Finally, it should be noted that if the 1982 and 1983 bills had not been enacted, 1983 taxes would have increased sharply and the state would not have developed a long-term debt.

Unlike other debtor states, Texas is not eligible for interest deferrals or reductions in FUT penalty taxes. The reason is that the state's 1982 UI legislation caused a reduction of 1983 tax effort compared to what was previously scheduled to take place. Texas avoided having a $1 billion tax increase in 1983. The previous tax schedule is the benchmark used in the 1983 Social Security Amendments for judging state tax efforts. As a consequence the debt is subject to full interest payments and Texas employers face FUT penalty taxes of .3 percent in 1985 and .6 percent in 1986. If the state economy rebounds rapidly in 1984 and 1985 it may obviate the need for 1986 FUT penalty taxes. Thus, the debt problem in Texas is on a much smaller scale and has been more easily remedied than in the four states with larger trust fund debts.

Wisconsin

Wisconsin was the first state to institute unemployment insurance. Its law passed in 1932, three years before the Social Security Act of 1935 which caused UI programs to be adopted by all the states. Wisconsin was among the first states to implement such innovative ideas as experience rating of individual employers, changing maximum benefit duration over the business cycle and indexing maximum weekly benefits.

During most of the program's history, important UI legislative proposals have originated with the Wisconsin Unemployment Compensation Advisory Council. This 11-member body which has 5 representatives from business, 5 from labor and is chaired by a nonvoting departmental employee serving as a public member has traditionally developed proposals using open procedures and receiving inputs from diverse economic interests within the state. Between 1932 and the mid-1970s, it was usually possible to balance the diverse economic interests of employers and employees within the Advisory Council to arrive at mutually acceptable UI legislation. The result was an innovative state program that successfully adapted to changing cyclical conditions. Its benefit structure could be termed liberal when compared to most states, but the program was not unusually expensive.

In the late 1970s, the labor and business policy positions at Advisory Council meetings became increasingly polarized as each side became less willing to make concessions in formulating needed UI legislation. Labor was unwilling to permit any benefit reductions and employer groups would agree to increases in UI tax schedules only if there were sharp benefit cutbacks. As a result an impasse developed at precisely the time when unemployment rose to unprecedented levels. During 1982 and 1983, Wisconsin borrowed $802 million, the first time loans were needed in the program's history. The scale of borrowing was so large that the state's debt was projected to reach $1.7 billion by the end of 1986 unless major legislation to restore fiscal balance was enacted.[32]

During the 1970s, benefit payments as a percent of total payroll in Wisconsin were nearly identical to the national average. Column 8 of table A6 shows the two percentages were respectively 1.16 and 1.15. Indicators of benefit availability and weekly benefit generosity, however, show that unemployed Wisconsin workers were paid at higher than average rates. The state ratio of insured-to-total unemployment exceeded the national ratio in 9 of 10 years while the ratio of weekly benefits-to-weekly wages was above average in all 10 years (see columns 10 and 11 respectively). Low unemployment in the decade offset the effect of these two high ratios. Between 1970 and 1979, the Wisconsin unemployment rate averaged 1.4 percentage points less than the national average and fell below the national rate in each of the 10 years. Thus, through the 1970s Wisconsin was able to provide its workers with generous UI benefits (e.g., no waiting week, maximum duration in excess of 26 weeks, indexed weekly benefits with the maximum changing twice per year) without imposing above-average costs on its employers.

Wisconsin entered the 1970s with a trust fund balance of $333 million (on January 1, 1970) and a reserve ratio multiple of 2.40, well above the 1.50 ICESA minimum standard. Reserves were drawn down somewhat during 1971 and 1972 but were then rebuilt to $300 million in 1973. Due to inflation, the reserve ratio multiple continued to decline somewhat in 1973 and 1974 but at the start of 1975 it still stood at 1.47, just below the recommended minimum actuarial standard.

When unemployment rose to 6.9 percent in 1975, trust fund reserves were quickly reduced to $120 million by the end of that year. As reserves dropped, the state responded by raising both employer tax rates and the taxable wage base (to $6,000) in 1976. Between 1976 and 1979 revenues exceeded benefit payments in each year and trust fund reserves were rebuilt to $465 million by the end of 1979. Although this was the highest amount of nominal reserves in the program's history, the reserve ratio multiple stood at only 1.06, an indication of how much inflation had occurred in the late 1970s.

Higher unemployment of 1980 and 1981 again quickly depleted the UI trust fund. Although actuarial projections from 1980 onward showed a clear need for loans, the Advisory Council was unable to agree upon a set of legislative recommendations. The labor members refused to accede to any benefit cuts, and business representatives would not agree to any tax increases until there were benefit cutbacks. Despite sharply higher unemployment in 1982 this impasse continued. For the year as a whole, benefit outlays exceeded tax revenues by more than $400 million. Payouts were 2.27 percent of total payroll, the highest payout rate for any year in the entire history of the program. Loans for this single year totaled $430 million.

In November 1982, a new governor was elected. After taking office in January 1983, Governor Earl moved quickly to break the impasse that had developed in the Advisory Council. He appointed a special panel of four (the Republican and Democratic leaders of the Assembly and Senate) with the Secretary of the Department of Industry, Labor and Human Relations named as the nonvoting chair. This group quickly developed a legislative package, made its recommendations in early April, and a bill was then enacted on April 15. The entire legislative process was conducted without input from the Advisory Council, something unique in the history of Wisconsin UI legislation.

Individual provisions of this legislation and estimated 1983-86 financial impacts were as follows.[33] (1) The weekly benefit maximum was frozen for four years at $196, its level on January 1, 1983 ($78 million). (2) Maximum potential duration of regular UI benefits was reduced from 34 to 26 weeks when insured unemployment falls below certain trigger thresholds ($82 million). (3) Provisions with respect to those who quit jobs (or refuse suitable work) were tightened. A "quit-to-take" (a new job) provision was added. To continue eligible for benefits under this provision, a claimant must work at least four weeks in the new job (which must be in covered employment) and must meet certain other conditions. Otherwise, a claimant who quits must work at least seven weeks in covered employment after the quit and earn at least 14 times the weekly benefit amount; the remaining benefits based on work for the quit employer are reduced by half. Under prior law, a person who voluntarily quit could requalify for full benefits by working four weeks and earning

$200, not necessarily in covered employment ($158 million).[34] (4) Those who are discharged for misconduct must requalify for benefits by working at least seven weeks in covered employment, with earnings at least 14 times the weekly benefit rate. Previously, only a three-week wait was required. As under prior law, all credit weeks with respect to the discharging employer are cancelled ($2 million). (5) Base period weeks of employment were raised from 15 in 1983 to 18 in 1984 and then to 19 in 1986. To qualify for benefits in 1984, a claimant needs base period earnings in covered employment of at least $1,646—18 weeks times the state average weekly wage ($304.80) times 30 percent. (The claimant meets this requirement even if the $1,646 is earned in 19 or more weeks.) There was no equivalent requirement in prior law. As before, benefit checks are not paid based on work for an employer where wages averaged $72 per week or less ($118 million).

There were several important changes in employer UI taxes. (6) The taxable wage base was raised to $8,000 in 1983, to $9,500 in 1984, and to $9,700 in 1986 ($449 million). (7) The tax rate schedule was revised upward from a 0-7.4 percent range in 1983 to a .4-8.5 range in 1984. The latter is the highest of four possible rate schedules (the lowest has a .1-5.4 percent range) and it will probably also apply in 1985 and 1986 as well ($189 million). (8) The cap on the maximum annual tax rate increase for covered employers was raised from 1 percent to 2 percent ($97 million). (9) The tax treatment of employers with large negative account balances was changed. Previously negative balances above a certain size were written off (like a bad debt). Under the new law, no writeoffs will be allowed in 1984 and 1985, and in later years they will be allowed only where the firm has paid the top rate for at least two years in succession (13 million). (10) Provisions permitting firms to "buy" a lower rate by making voluntary contributions exactly sufficient to move their balances into lower brackets were tightened by limiting such rate reductions to a single bracket and sharply reducing bracket size ($22 million). (11) Starting in 1984 payments for extended benefits were to be experience rated ($23 million). (12) A temporary surtax (8 percent of the basic tax) was levied in 1984 to avoid a 1984 FUT penalty tax. This tax increase will be offset by a one-year reduction in solvency taxes in 1986 ($32 million net revenue loss in 1984-86).

The Wisconsin legislation was projected to increase program solvency by over $1 billion during the four years from 1983 to 1986.[35] Over these four years it raised revenues by $761 million and reduced benefits by $438 million for a 63/37 division between state tax increases and benefits cuts. As a consequence, the state's UI debt at the end of 1986 was projected to be $600 million instead of $1.7 billion.

The 1983 Wisconsin bill was clearly influenced by the provisions of 1982 and 1983 federal UI legislation that affect debtor states. The changes in taxes and benefits will enable the state to avoid FUT penalty taxes on 1984 and 1985 payrolls. Also, the increase in net solvency is large enough to qualify the state both for 80 percent deferrals in 1983-85 interest payments and for (one percentage point) lower interest rates in 1983-85. The total resulting savings to Wisconsin employers in 1983-86 is $96 million in reduced FUT penalty taxes and $257 million in reduced and deferred interest charges.[36] When these savings are subtracted from the $761 million of tax increases projected under the 1983 legislation, the net employer tax increase becomes $408 million. Compared to benefit reductions of $438 million, the net tax change represents 48.2 percent of the combined net tax increase and benefit reduction. Thus, employers and workers will experience roughly a 50-50 split in the net change in program solvency over the 1983-86 period.

Wisconsin was able to act after devising a way to circumvent the deadlock in its Unemployment Compensation Advisory Council. The state has enacted a major bill that will substantially reduce future indebtedness. Even after the 1983 legislation, however, the state will still have a UI debt well beyond the end of 1986.

Louisiana

An unemployment insurance funding problem became apparent in Louisiana in 1982 when the state needed $102 million in federal loans. Unusually high benefit payments reflect continued increases in unemployment dating from late 1979. A downturn in petroleum production was the primary contributor to financing problems in this major energy-producing state. Further increases in unemployment during 1983 led to additional borrowing of $427 million. Thus a state that had never previously borrowed acquired an interest-bearing debt of nearly $500 million (or 2.2 percent of 1982 payrolls) in just two years.

Despite being an important energy-producing state, Louisiana has experienced above-average rates of unemployment in most years since 1970. During the 1970-79 decade, its unemployment rate averaged nearly a full percentage point above the national average, i.e., 7.1 versus 6.2 percent (see volumn 9 in table A7). Traditionally, UI in Louisiana has compensated a low proportion of the unemployed and weekly benefits have been lower than average. Columns 10 and 11 in table A7 display data showing below average ratios of insured to total unemployment and, through 1976, below average ratios of weekly benefits to weekly wages. In September 1976, however, a major liberalization of the weekly benefit statute became effective. The weekly benefit maximum was raised from $90 to $120 and was indexed to two-thirds of the state's average weekly wage. Since then, the ratio of weekly benefits to weekly wages has consistently exceeded the national average. Despite generally high unemployment since 1970 and generous weekly benefits since late 1976, Louisiana's benefit costs have been lower than average in most years. Between 1970 and 1982 the ratio of benefit payments to total payroll in Louisiana (column 8 in table A7) exceeded the national average in just four years. Unfortunately, 1982 and 1983 have been years of extraordinarily high benefit costs, the highest in the history of Louisiana's program.

Louisiana is not known for high employer UI taxes. Its tax base has never exceeded the FUT tax base and its average tax rates on taxable wages have never been unusually high for a sustained period. This situation prevailed in 1982 as unemployment rose and the state's trust fund was depleted.

Since 1970 there has been a rather steady downtrend in the Louisiana UI trust fund. As can be seen in column 1 of table A7, the state's reserve ratio multiple has declined in most years, with 1979 providing one important exception. Prior to 1983 employer UI tax rates were determined by a combination of their own reserve balances and the aggregate balance in the state trust fund. There were 10 different tax rate schedules, and the highest schedule became effective on the following January 1 if the June 30 trust fund balance fell below $125 million. The balance fell below this minimum threshold in 1978 causing tax rates to rise sharply in 1979. The range of rates shifted upward from .1-2.7 percent in 1978 to 1.63-4.53 percent in 1979, and the average rate on taxable wages (column 15) increased from 1.74 percent to 3.27 percent. Because of the higher taxes, the state trust fund balance increased by $114 million during 1979 (from $124 to $238 million) and the reserve ratio multiple rose from .46 to .77. Effective tax rates declined after 1979 and the trust fund balance gradually eroded in 1980 and 1981.

The increase in Louisiana's unemployment rate since 1980 has been particularly sharp. While the national unemployment rate rose from 7.1 to 9.6 percent between 1980 and 1983, Louisiana's rate jumped from 6.7 to 11.8 percent. The unusually severe state recession has been directly responsible for the accumulation of a substantial UI trust fund debt. Heavy layoffs in 1982 caused benefit outlays to rise sharply in that year and exhausted all the state's trust fund reserves.

Because the trust fund balance was below $125 million on June 30, 1982, Louisiana employees faced the prospect of sharply higher tax rates in 1983 when the 1.9-4.5 percent tax rate schedule was slated to go into effect. Additionally, because the debt was interest-bearing, there would also have to be new taxes to pay the required interest costs. Since 1982 benefit payments were much larger than tax revenues and an economic upturn was not taking place, it was obvious that large additional debts would accumulate unless corrective action was taken.

The primary reason for a special legislative session called in January 1983 was to address the state's UI funding problem. At the end of January, two bills were passed, one dealing with UI benefits and the other with taxes.[37] The tax changes were made retroactive to January 1, 1983 while the benefit changes became effective on April 3, 1983. At the time of their passage it was anticipated that the tax and benefit changes in conjunction with a strong economic recovery would cause the state's debt to be paid off by the end of 1986.

Individual provisions of the 1983 legislation were as follows.[38] (1) The weekly benefit maximum was frozen for an indefinite period at $205, the maximum in effect since September 1982. (2) Retroactive compensation for the waiting week was stopped. Previously the waiting week was compensated after a worker had received benefits for six

weeks. (3) The maximum potential duration of regular UI
benefits was shortened from 28 to 26 weeks. (4) The range of
experience rated tax rates was widened. Under the previous
statute, the range of rates in 1983 would have been from 1.9
to 4.5 percent. The new range was from .3 to 4.5 percent
with the maximum experience rated rate (for employers with
the biggest negative reserve balances) then rising in successive years and reaching 6.0 percent in 1986. (5) To help
repay the federal loans a solvency surtax was added for the
years 1983-1986. The surtax was to be a 20 percent add-on to
basic employer taxes in 1983 and up to 30 percent in later
years.[39] (6) A special surtax was instituted for employers
with chronic negative account balances. Those with negative
account balances on the June 30 tax computation date in two
successive years were subject to a special tax of 5 percent
which was added to their basic experience rated tax. (7) An
explicit tax to cover noncharged benefits (also called social
charges) was instituted. This too was computed as a proportional add-on to the basic experience rated tax rate. (8) An
interest surtax was added. It was levied on the previous
year's taxable wages at a single flat rate sufficient to cover
interest accruals on the previous year's debt. The 1983 rate
was .2 percent and it is anticipated that the 1984 rate will be
about .6 percent.

The Louisiana tax changes will lead to systematically
higher program revenues in the years after 1983. They also
have the effect of increasing the degree of experience rating.
In 1983, for example, the range of possible tax rates was increased from 2.6 percentage points under the previous law
(i.e., the 1.9-4.5 percent range of the preceding tax schedule)
to 5.3 percentage points (from 5.7 down to .4 percent). By
1986 this maximum range could be as wide as 7.9 percentage
points (from .4 to 8.3 percent),[40] about three times the range
of the pre-1983 tax rate structure. Because the tax changes
preempted a major increase in minimum tax rates previously

scheduled for 1983, however, actual 1983 tax revenues were somewhat lower than what would have been collected under the previous law. The average 1983 tax rate on taxable wages was about 3.3 percent, but it would have been close to 3.8 percent under the preceding law.[41]

Thus because tax effort declined relative to the standard provided by the previous law, Louisiana does not qualify for any of the interest deferral provisions of the 1983 Social Security Amendments. The state has opted for a somewhat smoother time path of average employer tax rate increases and greater degree of reliance on experience rated taxes to generate added revenues. Starting in 1985, Louisiana employers will also be subject to FUT penalty taxes.

Because the Louisiana economy did not recover in 1983, the state has continued to accumulate debts subsequent to its 1983 legislation. Under current (mid-1984) projections, all loans are expected to be repaid in either 1987 or 1988. Solvency surtaxes of 30 percent are expected for each of the years 1984-86. For the years 1985-87, FUT penalty taxes are expected to generate at least $160 million for loan repayments. Thus, Louisiana has taken action to improve UI program solvency, but net solvency was not improved by 25 percent in 1983 and the state did not qualify for the potential financial relief available under TEFRA and/or the 1983 Social Security Amendments.[42]

New Jersey

New Jersey's UI program experienced a serious funding problem in the mid-1970s. Between 1975 and 1978, loans in excess of $700 million were required and over $400 million was still outstanding at the end of 1983. The state economy has performed relatively well in the 1980s and there has not been a tendency towards chronic borrowing as in the previous decade. New Jersey still has a comparatively large debt (the debt of $476 million at the end of 1983 represented 1.0 percent of 1982 payrolls), but since 1980 it has been reduced by over $200 million. Because its debt is based on old (interest free) loans, recent New Jersey legislation has aimed to reduce FUT penalty taxes and has been influenced more by 1982 TEFRA provisions than by the 1983 Social Security Amendments.

Historically New Jersey has provided its residents with a high benefit/high tax UI program. During the 1949-59 and 1960-69 periods, benefits as a percent of total New Jersey payroll average 1.58 and 1.35 percent respectively as compared to national averages of 1.17 and 1.00 percent respectively. The differential was even wider in the 1970s when the New Jersey average was 1.91 percent while the national average was 1.15 percent (see column 8 in table A8). Between 1970 and 1979, the state's unemployment rate averaged a full percentage point more than the national average (7.2 versus 6.2 percent), and unemployment remained very high in 1976 and 1977 after the national economy recovered from the 1974-75 recession. Table A8 also shows that New Jersey compensates a relatively high proportion of its unemployed. The ratio of insured-to-total unemployment exceeded the national average in every year between 1970 and 1983. Thus high benefit costs in the 1970s reflect both high unemployment rates and high ratio of insured to total unemployment.

New Jersey entered the 1970s with a trust fund balance of $483 million and a reserve ratio multiple of 1.22. Reserves were largely depleted in 1971 and 1972 and not rebuilt in the next two years. Thus when unemployment rose sharply (to 10.2 percent) in 1975 the state quickly exhausted all reserves and had to borrow $352 million in that year alone (column 3). Additional loans of $383 million were then required in 1976-78. Continuing deficits occurred despite annual increases in the taxable wage base and increases in average taxes on taxable payroll to above 4 percent.[43] In New Jersey, taxes as a percent of total payroll in 1977 and 1978 were higher than in every other state except Alaska, Hawaii and Oregon. A deep and prolonged recession coupled with liberal UI benefit availability caused the state to borrow a total of $735 million despite imposing very high UI tax rates.

Accumulation of new debts has not been a problem for New Jersey in the 1980s. The state's unemployment rate has remained below the national average and it fell by 1.2 percentage points (from 9.0 to 7.8) in 1983. As a consequence, benefit payments as a percentage of payroll (though still higher than the national average) have averaged less in 1980-83 than they did for the decade of the 1970s. A second factor aiding program solvency in the 1980s has been the presence of an indexed taxable wage base. Since 1975, the wage base has been 54 percent of the state's average wage, reaching $9,600 in 1984. Indicative of improved solvency, the only loan required between 1980-1983 was a 1983 advance of $79 million that was repaid in the same year. Thus all of the state's UI debt continues to be the result of borrowing that occurred in the 1970s.

Loan repayments have been made at a slow pace. Voluntary payments of $40 and $43 million were made in 1978 and 1979 respectively, in lieu of FUT penalty taxes. Penalty taxes were first levied in 1981, and between 1981 and 1983 they accounted for $230 million in repayments. As noted, the 1983 loan was repaid in the same year.

Because New Jersey's debt is old debt and because the state has not experienced large deficits in the 1980s, there was less pressure to enact legislation immediately in 1983 to take advantage of financial provisions of the 1983 Social Security Amendments. The absence of large current deficits has meant that smaller scale adjustments could be made in comparison to states with much larger debts. Furthermore, the FUT penalty taxes provide an automatic mechanism for ensuring loan repayments. In 1983, a bill was proposed that would have improved program solvency and hastened the pace of debt reduction. Although that initiative was not successful, a similar bill was passed in March 1984 that raises taxes and causes a faster rate of loan repayment and a faster restoration of the UI trust fund.

New Jersey's 1984 legislation can be viewed as having two components; temporary measures to hasten debt repayment and rebuild the trust fund and longer run measures to improve the overall solvency of the program. Based on actuarial materials supplied by the state, it is estimated that the legislation will improve program solvency but by a rather modest amount during the 1984-87 period.[44] Temporary measures include a two-year 10 percent surtax on employers and a one-time transfer of monies from a state disability trust fund to the UI trust fund.[45] The permanent measures improve solvency by more than $50 million per year, but because of timing differences they do not start to have important effects until calendar year 1987. Permanent changes in benefits become effective in October 1984 whereas the permanent tax changes do not take effect until July 1986.

Individual provisions and their effects on program solvency during 1984-87 are as follows. (1) The formula for determining weekly benefits was modified. Previously, weekly benefits were two-thirds of base period weekly wages with a maximum equal to half of the state's average weekly wage. The new benefit formula lowers the replacement rate to .6, raises the weekly maximum to .567 of the state's weekly wage and pays dependents' benefits. For a single person, the weekly benefit maximum in 1984 was increased from $170 to $192. This change leads to increased benefit payouts ($104 million reduction in net solvency). (2) In calculating weekly benefits, future computations will round the benefit amount down to the nearest dollar ($23 million). (3) Base period earnings requirements were increased. In 1985 a worker will need 20 weeks of employment at weekly wages of at least 20 percent of the statewide average (or $71) rather than the current $30. Also, for workers with earnings concentrated in just a few weeks of the year the dollar amount for the alternative base period earnings requirement was raised from $2,200 to $4,100 ($62 million). On balance, the changes cause benefit payments to increase by $19 million over the 1984-87 period.[46]

Several tax changes were also made. (4) The employee tax rate on taxable wages was increased from .5 to .625 percent in July 1986 ($41 million). (5) A temporary surtax of 10 percent was added to employer taxes due between October 1984 and September 1986 ($147 million). (6) A one-time transfer of funds from the New Jersey Temporary Disability Insurance (TDI) fund to the UI trust fund will be made in 1985 ($50 million). (7) The range of employer tax rates was increased from 1.2-6.2 percent to 1.2-7.0 percent effective July 1986 ($34 million).

The total impact of the seven changes during 1984-87 will be a $253 million increase in program solvency. The employee share (increased employee taxes plus the transfer from the state disability trust fund[47] less the small net liberalization in weekly benefits) will be $72 million. The employer share (the temporary 10 percent surtax plus the increased maximum tax rate) is $181 million or 71.5 percent of the total.

This law raises the state's solvency in 1984-87 and helps qualify New Jersey employers for a cap on their FUT penalty tax rate. Although the state might have qualified for a cap in 1984 that would have maintained a .6 percent rate even without this law, it is more likely the rate would have risen to .8 percent (payable in 1985).[48] During 1985 and 1986, it is estimated that the savings in FUT penalty taxes, i.e., the .6 rather than the .8 percent rate, is about $85 million.[49] Since the debt will be repaid by the end of 1986, there will be no savings in FUT penalty taxes in 1987. When this $85 million FUT tax reduction is considered in calculating the net increase in program solvency for the 1984-87 period, the total change becomes a $168 million net increase and the employer share ($96 million, or $181 million less the $85 million FUT penalty tax saving) is 57.0 percent of the total.

As a consequence of its 1984 law, New Jersey has improved UI program solvency, enabling the state to repay its debt more quickly and rebuild its trust fund more quickly. Unlike other debtor states, weekly UI benefits have been increased somewhat while at the same time improving program solvency. This was possible because the program already has had a balance between revenues and benefits in the 1980s, and because the state does not have to contend with the costs of a large interest-bearing debt.

Minnesota

Minnesota's UI program has experienced financing problems in the 1970s and again in the present decade. The earlier debt, accumulated between 1975 and 1977, was fully repaid by the end of 1979. Despite FUT penalty taxes and required interest payments that are levied on the 1980s debt, the state has not yet found an acceptable way to make major improvements in program solvency and reduce its indebtedness. A 1984 legislative proposal to substantially revamp Minnesota's program was turned down in the legislature. At the end of 1983, the state has a $350 million debt (1.7 percent of 1982 total payrolls) and it faced the prospect of higher FUT penalty taxes and continued interest payments on a substantial share of its debt.

Although Minnesota is generally known as a generous state in the provision of social services, its UI program has traditionally been less costly than the U.S. national average. For example, during the 1970s UI benefits as a percent of payroll averaged 1.01 and 1.15 percent in Minnesota and in the U.S. respectively (see column 8 in table A9). Lower than average costs are largely accounted for by the state's generally low unemployment. Between 1970 and 1979 its unemployment rate averaged 4.7 percent while the national average was 6.2 percent. Column 9 in table A9 shows that the state's unemployment rate was below the national average in every one of the 14 years between 1970 and 1983.

The effects of low unemployment on benefit costs are partly offset by the state's rather liberal UI program. The ratio of insured-to-total unemployment in Minnesota typically exceeds the national average, and, since 1974, weekly benefits have replaced a higher than average fraction of weekly wages. The computation of the weekly benefit was substantially liberalized in the mid-1970s by two changes; raising the weekly benefit maximum from $85 in 1974 to $105 in 1975 and indexing the maximum to two-thirds of the state's average weekly wage after 1975. As can be seen from table A9 the ratio of weekly benefits to weekly wages has exceeded the national average in every year since 1974.

Despite its high weekly benefits and the high ratio of insured-to-total unemployment, Minnesota's benefit cost rates have usually been less than the national average. The effects of a liberal benefit structure have been offset by low unemployment rates. Thus in table A9, the only years when benefits as a percent of payroll (column 8) exceeded the national average were the years 1980-82. In 1982 benefits were 1.89 percent of payroll, the highest cost ratio in Minnesota since 1940 and higher than the national average of 1.72 percent.

For several years Minnesota has maintained a taxable wage base that exceeds the base for the Federal Unemployment Tax. This has helped to offset effects of a low average tax rate on taxable wages. During the 1970s, for example, the average state tax rate was 18 percent below the national average (column 15 in table A9). Between 1970 and 1982 the state's average tax rate was always lower than the national average.

Minnesota entered the 1970s with UI trust fund reserves of $120 million, but a reserve ratio multiple of only 1.11. Low reserves in 1970 represent the continuation of a generally low reserve position that had existed throughout the 1960s. Following earlier recessions in 1958 and 1960-61, the state did not raise taxes and/or restrict benefits by enough in the 1960s to rebuild the trust fund.[50] Between 1970 and 1975 the reserve ratio multiple (column 1) gradually declined (reaching .45 at the start of 1975). When unemployment rose to 5.9 percent in 1975 and 1976 the trust fund was soon exhausted and loans of $172 million were needed in the 1975-77 period. After its initial borrowing, Minnesota took steps to increase program revenues. The tax base was raised substantially in 1976 and 1977 and average tax rates on taxable wages were also increased. Finally, the trust fund was sufficiently rebuilt in 1979 that the state fully repaid the $172 million. At the start of 1980, however, the trust fund balance stood at only $70 million.

Increased unemployment in 1980 caused the state to need more loans. Loan demand was especially high in 1982 and 1983 when the unemployment rate rose to levels not experienced in the preceding decade. Because recent loans carry interest charges, the state repaid almost half of these in the year that they were obtained ($177 of $358 million). The repayment of 1980-82 interest-free loans has been limited to FUT penalty taxes which were first paid in January 1983. Thus, between 1980 and 1983 the state borrowed $550 million but repaid $200 million leaving a debt of $352 million at the end of 1983.

After borrowing substantial amounts in 1982 and early 1983, the Minnesota legislature enacted a bill during its 1982 session that was intended to improve program solvency. Three important provisions in the bill were the following. (1) The maximum weekly benefit amount was frozen at $184 effective June 30, 1982, and limited to $7 annual increases for each subsequent year through June 30, 1985. (2) The amount of weekly wages required to qualify for a base period week of covered employment was increased from $50 to 30 percent of the average weekly wage ($81 in 1982, $87 in 1983 and $94 in 1984). (3) The taxable wage base for employers was raised from $8,000 to 60 percent of the annual average wage ($8,300 in 1982, $9,000 in 1983 and $9,800 in 1984). These plus other changes were expected to balance revenues with benefit payments. When unemployment continued upward in late 1982, however, the state needed additional and larger loans even though these 1982 provisions were in place.

During 1983 and 1984, Minnesota has not been able to assemble a legislative package designed to further improve program solvency that can command majority support in the state legislature. A temporary surtax adding 10 percent to employer taxes in 1983 and 1984 was passed in 1983 to cover the interest costs on the state's debt. Legislation in Minnesota often closely follows recommendations of the Department of Employment Security Advisory Council, a body that has labor, management and public representatives. Throughout most of its history, the Advisory Council has been able to make unanimous legislative recommendations that have been subsequently enacted. In 1983, a recommended package did not command unanimous support within the council and did not pass in the legislature.

A 1984 legislative proposal that added provisions limiting benefits had unanimous council support and the backing of most employer organizations. The 1984 bill included a limitation on increases in maximum weekly benefits, a solvency tax to repay the debt, an extension of the temporary surtax and an increase in the maximum employer tax rate. Despite its strong backing, this bill was not passed. Opposition came from an effective group of employer representatives who wanted larger benefit reductions and smaller tax increases. Special issues not addressed by the bill also raised impediments to its passage.[51] Since the 10 percent employer surtax expired at the end of 1984 it would seem that Minnesota needs to consider UI legislation again in 1985.

Minnesota employers first paid FUT penalty taxes in 1983. The January 1984 payment was .6 percent of 1983 federal taxable wages. Penalty taxes on federal taxable wages in the following two years were to repay about three-fourths of the $204 million of outstanding debt remaining at the end of 1984. If no new borrowing takes place, voluntary repayments in 1985 and 1986 can be expected to eliminate the remainder of the state's debt. Minnesota and West Virginia are the only two of the ten largest debtor states that did not pass important solvency legislation between the end of 1982 and 1984. Although it appears that debt repayments will be completed by 1986 in Minnesota, much of this will have been the result of FUT penalty taxes. Under its current UI statutes, substantial trust fund accumulations do not appear to be in store for the state.

West Virginia

West Virginia has experienced a major UI funding problem in the 1980s that reflects the poor overall condition of the state's economy. Between 1980 and 1983 the state accumulated a UI trust fund debt of nearly $300 million (or 3.7 percent of 1982 payrolls). As coal production has declined the state's average unemployment rate has grown from 6.7 percent in 1979 to 18.0 percent in 1983. This 1983 unemployment rate was by far the highest in the U.S.[52] Persistently high and rising unemployment since 1979 explains how the state could accumulate a large debt while at the same time having among the highest average employer tax rates in the nation.

Traditionally, UI program costs have not been unusually high in West Virginia. Between 1949 and 1959, benefits as a percent of covered payroll did exceed the national average as the U.S. economy completed a major changeover from coal to oil in both commercial and residential usage. Since soft coal mining is the state's largest industry, West Virginia experienced a prolonged period of high unemployment and low growth from 1945 to 1959. This was responsible for a high rate of benefit payouts. During the next two decades, however, the state had UI benefit costs that were, in fact, below the national average. Table A10 shows that benefits as a percent of covered payroll (column 8) fell below the national average in every year between 1970 and 1977, and for the 1970-79 period they averaged .93 percent compared to a national average of 1.15 percent.

During the late 1970s, three developments led to rapid increases in UI benefit payments in West Virginia. First, there were liberalizations in the computation schedule used to determine weekly UI benefits. The weekly benefit maximum was raised from 67 to 70 percent of the state's average weekly wage in 1979, and in both 1978 and 1980 the replacement rate computation formula for high wage workers was liberalized. Second, the state increased the maximum potential benefit duration for regular UI benefits from 26 to 28 weeks effective in 1979. Third, and more important, state unemployment began to increase in 1979 and it increased in every subsequent year through 1983. As a result of these three developments, benefits were 3.01 percent of total payroll in 1982, the highest of any year since World War II and a higher percentage than in all other states except

Michigan and Pennsylvania. Because of benefit liberalizations and because many recent claimants have been high
wage coal miners, the ratio of weekly benefits-to-weekly
wages (column 11 in table A10) has risen from .290 in 1977
to .400 in 1982. Also, average duration in benefit status has
been higher in the 1980s than earlier because of the high
unemployment. Thus, since the mid-1970s, West Virginia
has become a state of chronically high UI benefit costs.

West Virginia first required UI loans in 1980. It borrowed
$47 million in 1980 and $53 million in 1981. After it became
clear that the state had a serious UI financing problem, a major bill was enacted in 1981 to increase program solvency. On
the benefits side, there were some increased restrictions on
benefit availability. Payments for partial unemployment
were reduced and several disqualification penalties were increased. The most important changes took place on the
revenue side of the program. The tax base was immediately
raised to $8,000. A surtax equal to 1 percent of taxable
payroll was added to each employer's contribution rate starting in 1981. This tax is to remain in effect until the UI trust
fund is restored to an adequate level (defined as equal to
average level of benefit payments for the preceding three
calendar years). Also, the range of experience rated tax rates
was widened substantially. Previously, rates ranged from 0
to 3.3 percent. Including the 1 percent surtax, the new range
was from 2.5 to 8.5 percent.[53] Finally, tax rates applied to
new employers and construction industry employers were
raised.

At the time of enactment it was felt that the 1981 legislation would restore balance between program revenues and
outlays. Because the 1981-82 downturn affected energy-
producing industries so severely, however, the state continued to experience deficits despite a major increase in tax
collections. Between 1980 and 1982, total contributions more

than doubled, from $79 to $166 million. Nevertheless, loans were still needed and in 1983 the loan total ($152 million) exceeded the sum for the preceding three years. As long as coal production remains depressed, it appears West Virginia will continue to experience UI trust fund deficits.

Debt accumulation has been so serious in West Virginia that a further set of benefit reductions and tax increases may be legislated in 1985. In mid-1983, a Special Commission on the Unemployment Compensation Trust Fund was formed. The Special Commission has three members each from the state senate, the state house of representatives, labor and industry, plus the director of the Governor's Office of Economic and Community Development and the UI Commissioner as an ex-officio member. The Commission is due to make legislative recommendations in January 1985.

Unlike other debtor states, West Virginia was under less pressure to make large adjustments in net solvency during 1983 and 1984 as it is not immediately liable for the full interest charges on its interest-bearing debt. Because it raised taxes in 1981 causing the 1982 tax rate on total payroll to exceed 2 percent, the state qualifies for 80 percent interest deferrals during 1983-85. The 2 percent tax rate threshold in 1982 was an alternative interest deferral eligibility criterion included in the 1983 Social Security Amendments.

Financial pressures to improve the program's fiscal balance will be increasing in the next few years. FUT penalty taxes were first payable in January 1983. Penalty rates for the first three years were .3, .6, and .7 percent of federal taxable wages. The exact rates in subsequent years are not known with certainty. Future increases will be smaller if new legislation is enacted. In 1986 and later years there will be no interest deferrals, while deferred amounts from earlier years will also fall due. Thus, to prevent further debt accumulation and to reduce future interest charges, it is clear that West

Virginia will be under strong pressure to enact a major UI legislative package early in 1985. Unlike the states with the largest debts, however, the inducement to enact legislation to improve the West Virginia UI program's solvency will be stronger in 1985 than it was in 1983 and 1984.

Debtor State Comparisons

The individual state experiences just described show a diversity of developments to be expected in the federal-state system of unemployment insurance programs. After the costs of borrowing increased in 1982, debtor programs were placed under greater financial pressure to repay debts and prevent the accumulation of sizeable new debts. The volume of loan repayments made in 1983 and 1984 (nearly $4 billion and $6 billion respectively) and the amount of debtor state legislation enacted between late 1982 and early 1984 both indicate a sharp break with the past. The 1983 Social Security Amendments provided an added spur to debtor state legislation by offering an explicit *quid pro quo;* reduced and/or deferred costs of debt in return for a major improvement in program solvency.

This section presents a comparative analysis of recent debtor state legislation. Although emphasis will be placed on common developments across the 10 debtor states, the fact of their diversity of circumstances and responses should not be downplayed. The following five examples provide good indications of debtor state diversity. (1) Minnesota did not develop a legislative package in 1983 or 1984 that could be enacted, despite accumulating a large interest-bearing debt. (2) West Virginia is able to defer most of its 1983-85 interest payments because of its 1981 legislation. Thus the pressure for new legislation to improve program solvency will be felt more acutely in 1985 and 1986 than it was in 1983. (3) New Jersey has been retiring debt in the 1980s and does not have to contend with interest payments. This helps explain why it was slower to act than most other debtor states. (4) When Texas and Louisiana acted in late 1982 and early 1983, one concern was a desire to retard sharp scheduled increases in employer tax rates. They had accumulated interest-bearing debts that required legislative remedies, but the tax provisions of their legislative responses precluded these two states from financial relief under the 1983 Social Security Amendments. (5) Sunset provisions were included in both the Illinois and the Ohio legislation. From the likely sizes of their debts in 1985-86, it seems clear that additional legislation will be required to ensure permanent improvements in program solvency. It would be simpler, but, also incorrect, to discuss the financing problem as if it were the same in all states.

Factors Related to Debt Accumulation

Although the general causes for the state UI funding problem were discussed in chapter 1, there are some additional considerations that become obvious after the individual debtor states have been studied. Table 2-2 presents state data related to three issues: low trust fund balances, liberalizations in weekly benefits, and unusually high benefit outlays in the 1980s.

The minimum reserve ratio multiple of 1.5 is a guideline that states can use in determining the adequacy of trust fund balances.[54] A state whose reserve ratio multiple falls below 1.5 is more likely than others to need federal loans following the onset of high unemployment. Columns 2, 3, and 4 in table 2-2 show reserve ratio multiples in the 10 states one, three, and five years before the year of their first loans (shown in column 1). Thus, for West Virginia, a state that first borrowed in 1980, reserve ratio multiples are shown at the start of 1979, 1977, and 1975. Not one of these 10 states had a multiple of 1.5 five full years prior to their first loan. For all 10 states, these pre-loan years can be characterized as

Table 2-2
Factors Related to Loans and Debt Accumulation in Ten Debtor States

State[a]	Year of first loan (1)	Reserve ratio multiple at the start of selected pre-loan years			Effect of weekly benefit liberalizations on average gross wage replacement rate			
		One year prior (2)	Three years prior (3)	Five years prior (4)	First full year of higher benefits (5)	Replacement rate in that year (6)	Two-year change in replacement rate (7)	Year of highest benefit cost rate 1947-82 (8)
Pennsylvania	1975[b]	.64	.98	1.24	1972	.424	.063	1982
Illinois	1975	.75	.60	1.17	1976	.412	.069	1982
Michigan	1975[b]	.57	.40	.85	1982	.415	.099	1958[c]
Ohio	1977	.37	1.06	1.07	1975	.400	.069	1982
Texas	1982	.40	.68	.55	1978	.302	.030	1958
Wisconsin	1982	.58	.93	.54	NA	NA	NA	1982
Louisiana	1982	.63	.46	.83	1977	.404	.058	1982
New Jersey	1975	.29	.57	1.22	NA	NA	NA	1975
Minnesota	1975	.61	.76	1.11	1976	.410	.021	1982
West Virginia	1980	.34	.54	1.10	1981	.366	.076[d]	1982

SOURCE: Data in columns (1)–(4) and (6)–(8) taken from *Unemployment Insurance Financial Data* (1984). Column (8) refers to benefits as a percent of total payroll. Column (6) refers to the ratio of average weekly benefits to average weekly wages. Column (5) based on the author's judgment about state law changes.

a. States are arrayed by the absolute size of their outstanding debt as of December 31, 1983.

b. This refers to the first loan after 1970.

c. The second highest benefit cost year was 1982.

d. This change refers to the four-year period from 1977 to 1981 because benefit liberalizations occurred in 1978, 1979, and 1980.

NA - Not applicable as there was no major liberalization of the benefit formula.

ones of low and/or declining reserve positions. Had actions been taken to increase trust fund balances when the multiples fell below 1.5, there would not have been much large-scale borrowing and debt accumulation in subsequent years.

Some readers may consider a minimum reserve ratio multiple of 1.5 to be too conservative a standard for judging trust fund adequacy. With the numerous and severe recessions experienced since 1969, there has been such a widespread loss of reserve adequacy that fewer and fewer states have met the 1.5 multiple standard. Even if a lower ratio of 1.0 were to be considered as minimally adequate, however, all states in table 2-2 still had inadequate reserve positions well before their first year of borrowing. Only one (Wisconsin's) of the 10-state multiples exceeded 1.0 three years prior to the year of their first loan. From these data it is hardly surprising that these particular states required loans.

One development that took place in most of the 10 debtor states before or at the time of their need for loans was a significant liberalization in weekly benefits. Columns 5-7 of table 2-2 identify the timing of benefit liberalizations in eight states and associated changes in gross replacement rates (average weekly benefits paid as a proportion of average weekly wages in covered employment). In six of the eight states the gross replacement rate rose by at least .058; percentage increases in this rate among the six ranged from 17 to 31 percent. These liberalizations significantly raised the ratio of weekly benefits-to-weekly wages and thus increased the amounts that the debtor states needed to borrow.[55]

The weekly benefit liberalizations noted in table 2-2 became fully effective in different years ranging from 1972 in Pennsylvania to 1982 in Michigan. Because they were spread out, their individual year-to-year effects on the U.S. average replacement rate in national data are not large. Table 2-2 shows only a small increase in the overall replacement rate between 1970 and 1982. When the individual states are examined, however, it becomes obvious that benefit liberalizations have contributed to the funding problems of several debtor states.

Finally, column 8 in table 2-2 shows that unusually heavy demands for benefits have been made in most debtor states in the 1980s. For seven of the ten, 1982 was the highest year of relative benefit costs for the entire period between 1947 and 1982. In Michigan 1982 was the second highest year of benefit costs for this 36-year period. The high benefit cost rate years shown in column 8 mirror the high unemployment rates shown previously in column 3 of table 2-1. Texas and New Jersey have had lower than average unemployment in the 1980s and this is reflected in table 2-2, i.e., their highest benefit cost rate occurred prior to the 1980s.

From the state data appearing in table 2-2, three factors are seen to contribute to funding problems in the ten states. (1) They had low trust fund balances for several years prior to their first loans. (2) Significant liberalizations in weekly benefits occurred prior to or at the time of their borrowing. (3) Due primarily to high unemployment, they have been faced with unusually heavy demands for benefit payments in the 1980s.

Sizes of Deficits and Sizes of Adjustments

Table 2-3 presents summary measures of debts, deficits in 1980-83 and the projected fund impact of recent legislation enacted in the ten states. Column 1 shows their outstanding debts at the end of 1983. To provide a sense for the scale of the individual UI programs and the extent of their recent fiscal imbalances, columns 2 and 3 respectively show annual averages of benefits as a percent of total payrolls for the years 1979-82 and the average annual increase in debt during 1980-83 expressed as a percent of total payrolls for 1979. For the U.S. as a whole, benefits averaged 1.29 percent of

Table 2-3
Debts and Effects of Recent Legislation to Improve UI Program Solvency, Ten Debtor States

State[a]	Debt outstanding December 31, 1983 ($000) (1)	Annual average Benefits paid as a percent of total payrolls 1979-82 (2)	Annual average Debt change (1980-83) as a percent of 1979 total payrolls (3)	Date of major UI legislation (4)	Average annual solvency change (1983-86) as a percent of 1982 total payrolls (5)	Eligibility in 1983-85 for: Deferral of interest (6)	Eligibility in 1983-85 for: Reduced interest rate (7)
Pennsylvania	2,617	1.66	.70	July 1983	1.18	1983-85	1983
Illinois	2,423	1.86	.64	April 1983	.75	1983-84	No
Michigan	2,322	2.27	1.27	December 1982	1.64	1983-85	1983-85
Ohio	1,976	1.85	.99	June 1983	.82[b]	1983-85	1983
Texas	685	.40	.29	May 1983	.32[c]	No	No
Wisconsin	626	1.61	.80	April 1983	1.12	1983-85	1983-85
Louisiana	476	1.33	.75	January 1983	.31[d]	No	No
New Jersey	422	1.72	-.17	March 1984	.14[e]	No[f]	No[f]
Minnesota	352	1.36	.51	NA	NA	NA	NA
West Virginia	288	2.15	1.05	1981	g	1983-85	No

SOURCES: Column (2) taken from U.S. Department of Labor, *Unemployment Insurance Financial Data* (1984). Columns (1), (3), and (5) are based on data from the U.S. Labor Department and the UI programs in the individual states. Calculations underlying columns (3) and (5) made at The Urban Institute.

a. States arranged by the absolute size of their outstanding debt as of December 31, 1983.

b. Average based on the three years 1983-85.

c. The tax increases refer just to taxes levied in 1983-86 to restore solvency to the Texas UI trust fund.

d. Based on estimates of tax increases and benefit reductions made at The Urban Institute.

e. Average based on the four years 1984-87.

f. New Jersey has no interest bearing debt.

g. West Virginia qualifies for 80 percent interest deferrals in 1983-85 because 1981 state legislation caused the ratio of taxes to total payroll to exceed 2 percent in 1982. This is the alternative criterion for obtaining interest deferrals.

NA - Not applicable as no major bill was enacted in 1983 or 1984.

payroll in the 1979-82 period. Thus seven of the ten states have paid unusually high amounts of benefits, with average payout rates ranging 1.61 to 2.27 percent of payroll. Louisiana and Minnesota have had somewhat above average benefit payout rates and Texas stands out for its very low rate of benefit payouts. As can be seen from column 3, nine of the ten states (all but New Jersey) increased their indebtedness in 1980-83. Like Pennsylvania and Illinois, New Jersey entered the 1980s with a large UI debt, but it reduced its debt by $230 million (from $652 to $422 million) in these four years. In eight states, annual debt accumulation during 1980-83 averaged at least .5 percent of total payrolls, and in three (Michigan, Ohio and West Virginia) it averaged 1 percent or more. Texas is again unusual in that it has had a low rate of debt accumulation compared to the other eight states with increased 1980-83 debts.

The timing of the recent UI legislation is shown in column 4. Five states enacted major bills between April and July 1983. Michigan and Louisiana had already enacted major legislation prior to April 1983.[56] In New Jersey and Minnesota, bills were introduced but not enacted in the 1983 legislative session. A New Jersey bill was subsequently passed in March 1984, but a 1984 Minnesota bill failed to be enacted. Only in West Virginia has there been no attempt to pass a major piece of UI legislation between December 1982 and mid-1984. However, it qualifies for 1983-85 interest deferrals because of unusually high 1982 tax rates that are partly the result of its 1981 legislation. Thus, eight of the ten states enacted major legislation between the end of 1982 and March 1984.

In five states (Pennsylvania, Illinois, Michigan, Ohio, and Wisconsin) the recent legislation will cause a large improvement in UI program solvency. Column 5 shows that the estimated average annual change in solvency (tax increases plus benefit reductions) for 1983-86, expressed as a percent of 1982 total payrolls, equals or exceeds .75 percent in these states. In each of the five, the change in program solvency compares favorably with the column 3 rate of debt accumulation experienced during 1980-83.

To qualify for the financial advantages offered by the 1983 Social Security Amendments, a state must make minimum improvements in "net solvency" with that term given a very specific meaning. The improvement in net solvency is measured as the sum of two percentage changes: (1) the percentage reduction in annual benefit payments compared to a baseline projection of benefits under the previous law and (2) the percentage increase in annual tax revenues compared to projected revenues under the previous law. If the sum of these two percentage changes is 25 percent in 1983, the state qualifies for a deferral of 80 percent of its 1983 interest payments. The required percentages of net solvency gains for interest deferrals rise to 35 and then to 50 percent in the two subsequent years. Even larger increases in net solvency (50, 80, and 90 percent in the first, second and third years respectively) qualify the state for a lower interest rate on its debts. Columns 6 and 7 show the states that qualify for interest deferrals and lower interest rates. Six qualify for interest deferrals[57] and four for lower interest rates. Five of the six that can defer interest are the same states where the column 5 percentage is at least .75 percent. Clearly, all five have benefited from the financial provisions of the 1983 Social Security Amendments. Only Illinois in this group fails to qualify for a lower interest rate sometime in the 1983-85 period.

The other three states with recent law changes (Texas, Louisiana, and New Jersey) also warrant additional comments. The scale of their net solvency adjustments is much smaller than in the five other states. In column 5, the adjustments as a percent of 1982 payroll range from .14 to .32 percent. Even though they do not qualify for favorable treatment of interest payments under the 1983 Social Security Amendments, these states can benefit from 1982 TEFRA provisions affecting FUT penalty taxes. New Jersey, in fact, will save on these taxes as a result of its 1984 legislation.[58] Since the state has only old debt, i.e., pre-1980 debt, there are no interest charges to be saved or deferred. Texas and Louisiana have interest-bearing debts. Both will reduce future indebtedness because taxes have been raised and/or benefits have been reduced. (In Texas, all of the adjustments have taken the form of tax increases.) However, as noted above, the tax increases resulting from bills passed in 1982 and 1983 will actually be lower in 1983 (and again in 1985 in Texas) than what would have occurred under the 1982 laws in effect when debts were first incurred. Thus the Texas and Louisiana tax changes represent tax reductions, i.e., reductions from previously scheduled tax increases, even though the average tax rate on employers will increase noticeably in both 1983 and 1984. Consequently, Texas and Louisiana do not qualify for interest deferrals.

Employer Tax Increases Versus Benefit Reductions

One of the issues addressed by recent legislation in eight of the debtor states is the ratio of employee sacrifices (benefit reductions and, in two states, employee tax increases) to employer sacrifices, i.e., higher employer taxes. Inability to resolve this issue in Minnesota is a major reason why the state did not enact important legislation in 1983-84. In the eight states there was a varied mix of employee and employer sacrifices. All enacted employer tax increases and seven (all but Texas) made benefit reductions.

For the eight UI programs table 2-4 shows that aggregate benefit reductions plus employee tax increases projected for the 1983-86 period were $3.7 billion and that employer tax increases were $8.2 billion. Thus the total change in solvency was $12.0 billion and the employer share was .689. Employer

Table 2-4

Tax Increases and Benefit Reductions Projected During 1983-86 Resulting from 1983 UI Legislation, Ten Debtor States

(Dollar amounts in millions)

State[a]	Employee benefit reductions (1)	Employer tax increases		Employer tax savings in 1983-86 due to 1983 legislation			Changes in program solvency		Employer share (ratio)	
		Gross (2)	Net (2)-(6) (3)	Interest costs (4)	Reduced FUT penalty taxes (5)	Total (4)+(5) (6)	Gross (1)+(2) (7)	Net (1)+(3) (8)	Gross (2)/(7) (9)	Net (3)/(8) (10)
Pennsylvania	805[b]	1,862	1,016	552	294	846	2,712	1,866	.687	.544
Illinois	780	1,160	630	389	141	530	1,940	1,410	.598	.447
Michigan	1,092	1,994	1,388	553	53	606	3,086	2,480	.646	.560
Ohio	351[c]	988[c]	532	411	45	456	1,339	883	.738	.602
Texas	0	1,161[d]	1,161	0	0	0	1,161	1,161	1.000	1.000
Wisconsin	438	761	408	257	96	353	1,199	846	.635	.482
Louisiana	139[e]	126[e]	89	37	0	37	265	228	.475	.390
New Jersey	72[b,f]	181[f]	96	0	85	85	253	168	.715	.570
Minnesota	NA	NA	NA	NA	NA	NA	NA	NA	NA	NA
West Virginia	NA	NA	NA	NA	NA	NA	NA	NA	NA	NA
Total	3,722	8,233	5,320	2,199	714	2,913	11,955	9,042	.689	.588

SOURCES: Estimates of benefit reductions and gross employer tax increases made at the time the legislation was enacted. Data in columns (1) and (2) obtained directly from the states. Columns (4) and (5) estimated at The Urban Institute. All other data derived from columns (1), (2), (4), and (5). Data measured in millions of dollars.

a. States arranged by the absolute size of their outstanding debt as of December 31, 1983.
b. Includes employee tax increases.
c. Data are for 1983-85.
d. The tax increases refer just to taxes levied in 1983-86 to restore solvency to the Texas UI trust fund.
e. Estimated at The Urban Institute.
f. Data are for 1984-87.
NA - Not applicable as no major bill was enacted in 1983 or 1984.

shares of the total change (column 9) ranged from 1.00 in Texas to .475 in Louisiana. Thus the relative political effectiveness of business and labor representatives in protecting their own constituents' interests varied considerably across the eight states.

Because of the 1983 legislation, debtor states were able to reduce 1983-86 interest payments and FUT penalty taxes. For the eight jurisdictions, total reductions were $2,913 million with $2,199 million in reduced interest payments[59] and $714 million in reduced FUT penalty taxes. Columns 4 and 5 in table 2-4 show the estimated dollar amounts for these two items in each state. If these savings had not occurred, employers in the debtor states would be required to pay higher payroll taxes during 1983-86. Thus the tax increases legislated in 1983 overstate the true increases in employer taxes that will occur in the 1983-86 period.

Column 3 shows net employer tax increases for 1983-86, the difference between the legislated increases and the savings on interest payments and FUT penalty taxes. The latter equal 35 percent of the legislated tax increases. Columns 8 and 10 then show net changes in program solvency and the employer share after recognizing these savings. For the eight states, the net increase in program solvency was $9.0 billion and the employer share was .588. In the individual states the employer share of the net change ranges from a low of .39 in Louisiana to 1.0 in Texas. The employer share of the aggregate sacrifice (benefit reductions plus tax increases) is thus reduced from .689 to .588 when these employer tax savings are recognized.

Table 2-4 shows that nearly $3 billion in interest charges and FUT penalty taxes will be avoided in 1983-86 as a consequence of solvency legislation in the debtor states. It should be emphasized that almost all of the relief is just a deferral of financial obligations, not an outright reduction in such obligations. Because FUT penalty taxes have been capped and interest payment schedules have been lengthened, both forms of repayment activities have only been delayed and will now entail increased state financial obligations in the period from 1987 to 1989. Should the overall economy experience another recession in the latter half of the 1980s, these deferred financial obligations will fall due at a most inopportune time.

Changes in Individual Program Provisions

To improve program solvency, all eight debtor states have enacted multiple changes in their statutes governing benefits and taxes. Table 2-5 shows the changes affecting weekly benefits, weeks per beneficiary, base period earnings requirements, disqualifications and employee taxes. Seven states enacted benefit reductions and two raised taxes on employees. At least three provisions were changed in each of the seven states. Thus the states have relied on multiple statutory changes in extracting sacrifices from employees.

The most common benefit changes were freezing maximum weekly benefits, lowering statutory replacement rates and requiring increased weekly earnings in computing base period credit weeks. Effects of these changes on average weekly benefits are already apparent. For the U.S. as a whole, average weekly benefits only increased from $119.34 in 1982 to $123.55 in 1983. The increase (3.5 percent) is the smallest percentage increase in weekly benefits since 1965. This low growth in weekly benefits is partly due to a slowdown in the overall rate of wage inflation. Also, however, many debtor states have frozen their weekly benefit maximums through the end of 1985 or 1986. Thus smaller overall percentage increases in weekly benefits will persist for at least two more years and will cause some reduction in the overall replacement rate.

Table 2-5
1983 Changes in UI Provisions Affecting Workers
in Seven Debtor States[a]

Provisions and change	PA	IL	MI	OH	WI	LA	NJ
Weekly benefit amount:							
Freeze maximum		X[b]	X	X	X	X	c
Lower replacement rate	X	X	X				X
Lower wage basis		X					
Round down weekly benefit					X		X
Regular duration of weeks payable:							
End retroactive payment of the waiting week	X			X		X	
Lower maximum duration payable	X				X	X	
Base period requirements (mimimum):							
Increase weeks of work (or high quarter or weekly benefit multiple)			X		X		
Increased earnings per week (or quarter or year)			X	X	X		X
Disqualifications:							
Stiffen penalties				X	X		
Employee taxes:							
Add or increase	X						X

SOURCE: Based on materials previously described in this chapter using state and other sources noted therein.

a. These are seven of the ten states with the largest debts as of December 31, 1983. The other three states did not change their benefit provisions in this period.

b. Maximum set at one level from April 1983 to January 1984 and then at a higher level from February 1984 to June 1986.

c. Maximum weekly benefits were increased under New Jersey's legislation.

Multiple changes were made in all eight states in employer tax provisions. Table 2-6 displays important tax changes by state. Five raised the taxable wage base per employee and all made changes in tax rates. Typically, flat rate taxes and percentage surtaxes, as well as a wider range of experience rated tax rates, were all affected by the legislation.

Table 2-6
1983 Changes in Employer UI Tax Provisions
in Eight Debtor States[a]

Provision and change	PA	IL	MI	OH	TX	WI	LA	NJ
Higher taxable wage base	X	X	X	X		X		[b]
Higher taxes:								
Flat rate taxes	X	X		X	X	X	X	
Percentage surtaxes	X	X			X	X	X	X
Increased range of tax rates	X	X	X	X	X	X	X	X
Higher taxes for negative balance employers:								
Modify tax rate limiters			X			X		
Increased account building taxes	X		X					
Eliminate writeoffs of negative balances						X		
Surtax for negative balances			X				X	

SOURCE: Based on materials previously described in this chapter using state and other sources noted therein.

a. These are eight of the ten states with the largest debts as of December 31, 1983. The other two states did not change their tax provisions in this period.

b. State has an indexed taxable wage base that was not affected by its recent legislation.

Although five debtor states raised the taxable wage base, they did not go that far above the federal taxable wage base and not one of the five indexed its wage base. In 1985, while the current FUT tax base of $7,000 is still slated to be in effect, the five state maximums will be as follows: Pennsylvania-$8,000; Illinois-$8,500; Michigan-$9,000; Ohio-$8,000; and Wisconsin-$9,500. Not one will have reached $10,000 by 1985. Since all five are high wage states, they will continue to tax less than half of all covered wages even after the increases in their taxable wage bases. This could contribute to renewed problems of revenue inadequacy in future years.

A controversial issue in nearly all states was how the burden of tax increases was to be allocated between employers with positive and negative account balances.[60]

Many researchers and others with a policy interest in state UI programs feel that a greater degree of reliance should be placed on experience rated employer taxes. A provision of TEFRA enacted in 1982 called for all states to have a maximum employer tax rate of at least 5.4 percent by 1985. These considerations would lead one to expect debtor states to raise maximum employer tax rates and make other changes to increase the degree of experience rating. One manifestation that experience rating has become more pervasive would be higher taxes on employers with negative account balances. Table 2-6 shows that such changes were enacted in 1983 in Pennsylvania, Michigan, Wisconsin, and Louisiana. Michigan in particular made three changes to increase taxes on negative balance employers. By avoiding very large flat rate surcharges in their 1983 legislation, it seems clear that Texas and Louisiana have increased their degree of experience rating. Because five of the debtor states in table 2-6 raised their taxable wage base, this change will also help the states to impose higher effective tax rates on employers with low and negative balances. This too can enhance the effective degree of experience rating.

A full assessment of the experience rating issue cannot be made here, but table 2-7 presents some useful summary data on recent changes in minimum and maximum employer tax rates in all 10 debtor states. The table covers the years 1978, 1982 and 1986. Only three states changed minimum tax rates between 1978 and 1982 (Pennsylvania, Illinois, and West Virginia), and in each the change was the result of legislation enacted in 1980 or 1981. Between 1982 and 1986, however, four states will have raised minimum rates. The 1986 minimum rates will be 2 percent or higher in only two states (Pennsylvania and West Virginia) and the arithmetic average of the ten is only 1.15 percent.

Maximum tax rates will increase measurably between 1978 and 1986 with much more than half of the total of the change

Table 2-7
Minimum, Maximum and Range of Employer Tax Rates
1978, 1982 and 1986

State	Minimum tax rate[a] (percent)			Maximum tax rate[a] (percent)			Range of experience rated tax rates (max.-min.) (percent)		
	1978	1982	1986	1978	1982	1986	1978	1982	1986
Pennsylvania	1.0	2.5	2.0	4.0	6.6	9.7	3.0	4.1	7.7
Illinois	.1	.6	.8	4.0	5.7	7.3	3.9	5.1	6.5
Michigan	1.0	1.0	1.0	7.5	9.0	10.0	6.5	8.0	9.0
Ohio	1.1	1.1	1.8[b]	4.8	4.8	7.0[b]	3.7	3.7	5.2[b]
Texas	.1	.1	.4	4.0	4.0	8.1	3.9	3.9	7.7
Wisconsin	.5	.5	.4	6.5	7.4	7.9[c]	6.0	6.9	7.5[c]
Louisiana	.1	.1	.4	2.7	3.4	8.3	2.6	3.3	7.9
New Jersey	1.2	1.2	1.2	6.2	6.2	7.0	5.0	5.0	5.8
Minnesota	1.0	1.0	1.0	7.5	7.5	7.5	6.5	6.5	6.5
West Virginia	0	2.5	2.5	3.3	8.5	8.5	3.3	6.0	6.0
Simple average of ten states	.61	1.06	1.15	5.05	6.31	8.13	4.44	5.25	6.98

SOURCES: Data for 1978 and 1982 taken from U.S. Department of Labor, "Comparison of State Unemployment Insurance Laws," July 1979 and January 1983 issues. 1986 data obtained from the individual states and based on current projections of maximum tax rates.

a. Minimum and maximum rates for 1986 exclude state taxes designed to pay the interest charges on UI debts. Interest taxes will be present in Pennsylvania, Michigan, Texas, Wisconsin, Louisiana and Minnesota.

b. These rates for 1985 are assumed to apply in 1986.

c. A temporary tax rate reduction in 1986 reduces the maximum tax rate from 8.5 to 7.9 percent and reduces the range of tax rates from 8.1 to 7.5 percentage points.

occurring after 1982. Note that seven of the maximum rates already exceeded 5.4 percent in 1982, three years before they are mandated under TEFRA to reach this level. By 1986 the lowest of these state maximum rates will be 7.0 percent, a full 1.6 percentage points above 5.4 percent. Thus the increase in the required maximum rate does not appear to have affected these debtor states in an important way.

Recent state legislation clearly has increased the range of experience rated tax rates. In the eight states with recent legislation, the range of rates in 1986 is wider than in 1982 and in three (Pennsylvania, Texas, and Louisiana) the increased range is at least 3 full percentage points. From table 2-7 it is clear the recent legislation has definitely increased the potential degree of experience rating and probably the actual degree as well. A more definitive conclusion would require an examination of micro data on employer tax rates.

Summary

By requiring interest payments on new loans made after March 31, 1982, the 1981 Omnibus Budget Reconciliation Act significantly increased the costs of UI debts. The 1983 Social Security Amendments offered debtor states a *quid pro quo:* the ability to reduce and defer the costs of debt in return for enacting legislation to improve UI program solvency. From the events described earlier in this chapter, it is clear that most debtor states responded by enacting major legislative packages that raised taxes and reduced benefits.

Because debtor UI programs have enacted major changes to improve fiscal solvency, they will be less likely to incur future debts. It is also clear that when future debts are incurred they will be repaid much more quickly than they were in the 1970s. A major change in repayment behavior is already evident in the 1983 and 1984 repayment data shown in table 1-3 of chapter 1.

To achieve improvements in program solvency, debtor states have enacted mutiple changes in both their tax and benefit statutes. In the aggregate, the shares of the total sacrifice in eight large debtor states for the 1983-86 period are roughly 69 percent employer tax increases and 31 percent benefit reductions. These respective percentage shares change to 59 and 41 percent when other employer tax savings gained in the period due to improved solvency (reduced FUT penalty taxes and reduced and deferred interest payments) are considered. It also appears that the recent legislation will cause these UI programs to place a greater degree of reliance on experience rated employer taxes.

In the future, state UI programs will be more financially self-reliant and there will be less federal monies involved in benefit provision, i.e., fewer loans to debtor UI programs, faster debt repayment and fewer EB benefit payments. This is a change desired by the Reagan administration. Their 1981 legislative initiatives are largely responsible for this change in behavior at the state level.

NOTES

1. Both types of debt measures are important. Absolute debt shows where the macro debt problem resides. Relative debt is useful for showing which states are apt to have more difficulties in repaying their loans.

2. The 1980 Pennsylvania legislation is described by Runner (1981).

3. Tax rates would have risen even more in 1980-82 if Pennsylvania hadn't allowed experience rated employers to deduct their FUT penalty taxes in the determination of the flat rate UI taxes owed to the state. If this deduction feature had not been present, average state tax rates (column 15 of table A1) would have been between 4.7 and 4.8 percent in the 1980-82 period.

4. See McCormick (1983).

5. See State of Pennsylvania (1983), p. 13. These estimates are based on data taken from the October 1983 forecast for the State of Pennsylvania made by Chase Econometrics Inc. Using an earlier January 1983 Chase forecast, the total change in program solvency for the 1983-86 period was estimated to be $2,798 million, somewhat larger than the estimate based on the October forecast ($2,712 million).

6. These estimates were made at The Urban Institute.

7. For background on the 1975 Illinois legislation see Becker (1981), pp. 33-36.

8. For the three-year period 1980-82, benefits were 1.98, 1.89, and 2.42 percent of total payroll respectively. The highest previous benefit payout rates were 1.75 percent in 1975, 1.70 percent in 1958, and 1.69 percent in 1976.

9. See Runner (1982).

10. People in Illinois have argued that an important reason for having the sunset provision was the uncertainty about how the legislation would affect benefits and revenues. The sunset provision ensures that after experience accumulates under the new law there will be a need to evaluate its effects and an opportunity to remedy any defects found in its actual operation. It could also be argued that the sunset provision reflects the poor understanding of many in Illinois about the seriousness of the state's UI funding problem and wishful thinking that the debt will go away by mid-1986.

11. The exact level of these maximum rates will be determined after state benefit experiences are known. As of mid-1984 it seems the actual maximums will be at or near the top of these ranges. The top rate for 1984, for example, is 6.3 percent.

12. The legislation also created a tax incentive to encourage employment retention (termed an Employment Incentive Program). Under this program an employer with years of bad layoff experiences could potentially reduce UI taxes. If such employers reduced layoffs and raised total employment, maximum tax rates could decline. This provision could have a measurable effect on tax revenues in 1986 and later years (after years of bad experience are eligible for removal from the time period used for tax rate computations) but it is still too early to assess how large the effect may be.

13. There is also a question about the breakdown between tax increases and benefit reductions. Some have suggested the actual breakdown of

sacrifices is closer to 50-50 than to the 60-40 split shown in publications issued by Illinois. The actuarial estimates used here are the data released to the public at the time of the 1983 legislation. See State of Illinois (1983).

14. These estimates were made at The Urban Institute.

15. See Blaustein (1981) for a description of this 1980 law.

16. Employer representatives felt there would be substantial savings to offset much of the extra costs arising from higher weekly benefits. Note in column 10 of table A3 that the ratio of insured-to-total unemployment did fall sharply between 1980 and 1981. The decline is partly the result of the 1980 legislation, but also it reflects benefit exhaustions. It is not clear what part of this decline should be attributed to the 1980 bill.

17. These calculations were made assuming that weekly benefits in 1981 and 1982 averaged $102, i.e., their 1980 level.

18. See chapter 3 in Blaustein (1982).

19. See State of Michigan (1983) for a summary of the legislation. The Bureau of Research and Statistics of the Michigan Employment Security Commission estimated the effects on benefits and revenues.

20. This estimate was made at The Urban Institute.

21. In fact the 1982 Michigan law was one factor behind the debtor state financial relief provisions included in the 1983 Social Security Amendments.

22. This estimate was made at The Urban Institute.

23. See Hemmerly (1983) for a description of important provisions in both bills and estimates of their effects on revenues and benefit payments during 1983-85. The sunset provision in the 1983 Ohio legislation partly reflects continued employer optimism about future growth, hence less need for long-run legislative remedies.

24. Hemmerly (1983).

25. Included in the total tax increases are small amounts raised by taxing new employers at a higher rate and increasing the interest penalty on delinquent tax payments. Also, there was a small benefit reduction ($13 million) caused by changing the requalification provision for workers who quit their jobs voluntarily.

26. These estimates were made at The Urban Institute.

27. This projection was made in early 1983.

28. For a description of the 1982 bill see Texas Research League (1982).

29. State of Texas (1983), p. 3.

30. See Texas Research League (1983).

31. Estimates of revenues generated by the 1983 UI legislation are based on projections of taxable wages and average tax rates that appear in Arthur Anderson and Co. (1983).

32. Projections of potential future indebtedness appear in table 6 of State of Wisconsin (1983).

33. The actuarial estimates published by the State of Wisconsin (1983) show effects of changing individual provisions while holding all others constant. As a consequence, the sum of their effects on benefits exceeds the total for all benefit changes. The estimates shown here have been deflated so that their sum agrees with the total estimated cutback in benefits.

34. Data provided by Clifford Miller, Wisconsin Department of Industry. Subsequent experience in Wisconsin under the new quit provisions suggests this estimated savings in benefit outlays is too large.

35. See State of Wisconsin (1983).

36. See State of Wisconsin (1983), table 26.

37. Major provisions of the 1983 legislation are described by Runner (1984).

38. No data have been found to show the budgetary effects of the individual changes or of the entire 1983 Louisiana legislative package.

39. After all loans have been repaid there will continue to be a surtax provision in the state's law. A surtax of 10 percent will be levied in any year when the trust fund balance as of the previous June 30 falls below $400 million.

40. This projected range is built up from the sum of three separate taxes; (i) the basic experience rated tax (.3-6.0 percent), (ii) a 30 percent solvency surtax (.09-1.8 percent) and (iii) taxes for social charges (.03-5.0 percent), after rounding to the nearest tenth of a percentage point.

41. An estimate of 3.8 percent under the previous law was made at The Urban Institute based on the time series pattern of earlier data, par-

ticularly the pattern of changes in tax rates between 1978 and 1979 when tax rates moved to the highest tax rate schedule under the previous law.

42. Louisiana has not published estimates of the increases in program solvency resulting from its 1983 legislation. Rough estimates made at The Urban Institute show taxes to be $126 million higher and benefits to be $139 million lower during 1983-86 as a result of the legislation. Net solvency is estimated to be 5 percent lower in 1983 but then 17, 26, and 29 percent higher in the next three years.

43. In 1977, for example, taxes were 4.15 percent of taxable payroll. New Jersey taxes covered employees at a flat .5 percent rate as well as taxing employers. Thus the 4.15 average percentage rate consists of a .5 percent tax on employees and an average 3.65 percent tax on employers.

44. These estimates were made at The Urban Institute using information supplied by the State of New Jersey.

45. New Jersey has a Temporary Disability Insurance (TDI) program that is financed by employer and employee contributions. Monies were transferred from the TDI trust fund to the UI trust fund.

46. Some other benefit provisions were also changed but their financial effects were too small to be estimated.

47. When New Jersey's TDI program was originally established, a TDI trust fund was created by transferring $50 million from the UI trust fund. The transferred monies were employee UI tax contributions. Thus, the transferral of the $50 million back to the UI trust fund should be considered as employee taxes.

48. In the absence of 1984 legislation, New Jersey might have qualified for a freeze in its FUT penalty tax rates at .6 percent under the four TEFRA conditions for a tax rate freeze.

49. This estimate was made at The Urban Institute.

50. State officials have offered two reasons why trust fund balances were not increased to higher levels: (i) the availability of interest-free loans from the U.S. Treasury and (ii) concerns by employers that a substantial accumulation in the trust fund could lead to further benefit liberalizations.

51. Two were the compensation of school bus drivers employed by private bus companies and compensation of permanent part-time workers who are laid off. Both issues affect small numbers of beneficiaries.

52. Michigan's 1983 unemployment rate of 14.2 percent was the second highest among all the states.

53. West Virginia has four tax rate schedules for its experience rated tax rate, all with a maximum rate of 7.5 percent but with minimum rates ranging from 0 to 1.5 percent. Thus the range of experience rated tax rates can be from 6.0 to 7.5 percentage points. The widest range applies when the trust fund balance exceeds 150 percent of average benefit costs for the preceding three years.

54. Recall that the reserve ratio multiple is the ratio of two ratios; the trust fund balance (as proportion of covered wages and salaries in the current year) divided by benefit payments for the previous highest cost year (as a proportion of that year's covered wages and salaries).

55. Replacement rates are known to increase in recessions. Thus some of the increases reflected in column 7 of table 2-2 could be linked to the business cycle. To determine that the cyclical effects are small the reader should examine column 11 in tables A1-A10. In no state did the replacement rate return to (or come close to) its previous level in later years following the benefit liberalization.

56. The Texas legislation of September 1982 and Ohio legislation of December 1982 were also intended to address their states' financing problems, but did not.

57. All but West Virginia qualify for interest deferrals on the basis of their 1983 (December 1982 in Michigan) legislation.

58. Its FUT penalty tax rate for the 1985 and 1986 payments is .6 percent rather than .8 percent.

59. The deferred interest payments in 1983-85 will have to be repaid, but the deferrals will presumably cause the payments to fall due in years of improved state finances and higher employer profit rates.

60. A negative balance employer is one whose cumulative benefit payments (measured from the date of initial UI coverage) exceed cumulative tax contributions.

3
Conditions of Debt Avoidance

Although 37 of 51 state UI programs needed federal UI loans some time between 1972 and 1983, prolonged and large-scale indebtedness has been avoided in most states. The factors or events that lead to a state's need for UI loans can be grouped into two broad categories: controllable and uncontrollable. Individual states can do very little to control their unemployment rate or their rate of economic growth. At any point in time the UI trust fund balance, which mirrors both past policy actions affecting program solvency and past economic events must also be taken as a given. What the state can control are the statutory provisions and administrative practices that affect UI revenues and benefit payments.

The present chapter examines general issues related to debt avoidance. Of the three uncontrollable factors (unemployment, economic growth and the current trust fund balance), the latter two are to be discussed. Unemployment has already received attention in chapters 1 and 2. The importance of active UI policy responses is to be emphasized here. The plan of the analysis is to start with one of the uncontrollable factors, trust fund balances as of 1969. Next, active policy responses are examined. In addition to summarizing the range of responses, one particular response, tax base indexing, is singled out for special attention. After the effects of economic growth on trust fund balances are discussed, the chapter concludes with a few summary observations.

The analytic approach to be followed in the chapter is to review selected data from all 51 jurisdictions and try to identify the characteristics of state programs that are associated with successful debt avoidance or the avoidance of large scale borrowing. The analysis is descriptive and the conclusions will be more tentative than definitive, because some states continued to borrow in 1984, because legislation to strengthen fiscal solvency may yet occur in 1985, and because with lags in data availability, information on state adjustments to their financing problems in the early 1980s is still incomplete. Therefore, the analysis will focus heavily on the developments in the 1970s as well as events of the present decade.

To place the UI borrowing and debt accumulation of the individual states during the 1970s and 1980s into a common perspective, table 3-1 displays selected data on borrowing. As noted, 37 jurisdictions borrowed at least once between 1972 and 1983, and loans are shown for two periods, 1972-79 and 1980-83. For both periods the tables shows the absolute amount of loans obtained and loans measured as a percentage of total payrolls.[1]

During the 1970s, loans were made to 23 programs but only 10 required amounts that exceeded $100 million (column 1). When loans are measured relative to the size of each state's total payroll (column 2) there are 13 states where loans exceeded 1 percent of 1975 payrolls and 7 of these states are located in the North East region. In 1980-83, loans were made to 29 states but only in 13 did the total exceed 1 percent of 1979 payrolls (column 4). Among this group of 13, 6 were located in the North Central region. Using 1 percent of total covered wages to define large relative loan amounts, roughly one-quarter of the states needed large

Table 3-1
UI Loans to Individual States 1972-79 and 1980-83
and Outstanding Debt as of December 31, 1983 (37 States)

State	Loans in 1972-79		Loans in 1980-83		Debt outstanding as of Dec. 31, 1983 ($ millions) (5)
	Amount ($ millions) (1)	Percent of total 1975 payrolls (2)	Amount ($ millions) (3)	Percent of total 1979 payrolls (4)	
Total: 37 states[a]	5,532	1.0	14,903	1.6	13,279
Alabama	57	.8	56	.5	
Arkansas	30	.8	118	1.8	86
Colorado			150	1.2	113
Connecticut	514	5.0	64	.4	280
Delaware	47	2.4	25	.9	44
District of Columbia	74	2.2	34	.8	64
Florida	42	.2			
Hawaii	22	1.0			
Illinois	946	2.5	2,547	4.4	2,423
Indiana			64	.3	
Iowa			253	2.4	127
Kentucky			250	2.1	151
Louisiana			528	3.3	476
Maine	36	1.8	1	.0	
Maryland	63	.6			
Massachusetts	265	1.6			
Michigan	624	2.3	3,044	6.7	2,322
Minnesota	172	1.6	550	3.2	352
Missouri			143	.7	90
Montana	10	.8	9	.3	9
Nevada	8	.4			
New Jersey	735	3.3	78	.2	422
New York	336	.6			
North Dakota			17	.9	
Ohio	2	.0	2,310	4.6	1,976
Oregon	18	.3			
Pennsylvania	1,222	3.6	2,587	5.2	2,617
Rhode Island	111	4.0	18	.5	90
South Carolina			6	.1	
Tennessee			60	.4	
Texas			803	1.3	696
Utah			29	.6	
Vermont	48	4.8	11	.7	25
Virginia			46	.2	
Washington	149	1.6			
West Virginia			302	4.3	291
Wisconsin			802	4.1	626

SOURCE: Data on loans in columns (1) and (3) based on materials supplied by the U.S. Department of Labor. Payroll data used to compute columns (2) and (4) were taken from U.S. Department of Labor, *Unemployment Insurance Financial Data* (1984). Column (5) based on U.S. Department of Labor, "Title XII Advance and Repayments as of December 31, 1983," January 9, 1984.
a. The 14 states which did not borrow in either period were: Alaska, Arizona, California, Georgia, Idaho, Kansas, Mississippi, Nebraska, New Hampshire, New Mexico, North Carolina, Oklahoma, South Dakota, Wyoming. Washington and Wyoming borrowed in 1984.

loans in 1972-79 and one-quarter again in 1980-83. Only four states (Illinois, Michigan, Minnesota and Pennsylvania) needed loans that exceeded 1 percent of payrolls in both periods. Column 5 of table 3-1 shows the amount of each state's debt as of the end of 1983. The 10 with the largest debts have already been individually examined in chapter 2. Despite the large number that borrowed during the 12-year 1972-83 period, most states have avoided accumulating major debts, including 14 that required no loans at all.

Initial Trust Fund Balances and Effective Tax Rate Increases

Perhaps the two most obvious explanations for debt avoidance are: (1) that some states entered the 1970s with much higher trust fund reserves than others and (2) that some states have been quicker to react to declining reserves and to raise employer taxes by substantial amounts. Table 3-2 presents information on trust fund balances at the start and end of the 1970s. Three groups of states are identified: the 14 that did not borrow between 1972 and 1983 (see footnote (a) of table 3-1), the 10 whose loans in the 1970s exceeded $100 million (see column 1 of table 3-1)[2] and the 27 other states. The distributions of reserve ratio multiples at the end of 1969 and 1979 are shown in the body of table 3-2 along with the medians of each distribution. The arrangement of the three subgroups of states from left to right in the table is a rough indicator of borrowing needs, i.e., from the smallest to the greatest needs.

Entering the 1970s, the three groups of states had systematic differences in their trust fund balances. The median reserve ratio multiple for the 14 nonborrowing states (2.50) was nearly double the multiple for the 10 with the largest loans (1.44). Ten of the former group had multiples of 2.0 or larger while six of the latter had multiples below the minimum 1.5 level recommended as adequate.

Table 3-2
Distribution of States by Year-End Reserve Ratio Multiples 1969 and 1979; States Grouped by Borrowing Characteristics

Period and reserve ratio multiple	All states	Did not borrow 1972-1983[a]	All other states[a]	Ten largest borrowers in 1970s[a]
	Number of states by borrowing characteristics			
Total	51	14	27	10
End of 1969				
Negative	0	0	0	0
0-.49	0	0	0	0
.50-.99	1	0	0	1
1.00-1.49	15	2	8	5
1.50-1.99	14	2	9	3
2.00-2.99	13	6	6	1
3.00 and above	8	4	4	0
Median[b]	1.84	2.50	1.80	1.44
End of 1979				
Negative	9	0	4	5
0-.49	12	0	7	5
.50-.99	17	4	13	0
1.00-1.49	11	8	3	0
1.50-1.99	2	2	0	0
2.00-2.99	0	0	0	0
3.00 and above	0	0	0	0
Median[b]	.63	1.19	.60	.00

SOURCE: Year-end 1979 reserve ratio multiples taken from U.S. Department of Labor, *Unemployment Insurance Financial Data* (1984): year-end 1969 multiples computed at The Urban Institute based on data from the same source.

a. The identity of individual states within the three groups is indicated in footnote (a) of table 3-1 and column (1) of table 3-1. The ten largest borrowers are states that borrowed in excess of $100 million between 1972 and 1979.

b. Computed at The Urban Institute.

The level of initial reserve ratio multiples is clearly associated with state borrowing in the 1970s. Sixteen states had multiples below 1.5 and 13 needed loans sometime during the decade. In contrast, only 3 of the 21 states with initial multiples of 2.0 or larger (the District of Columbia, Florida, and Washington) needed any loan and only Washington required a loan in excess of $100 million (although loans to the District of Columbia did represent 2.2 percent of 1975 payrolls). Thus, low initial reserves were one important factor determining the need for loans in the 1970s.

The bottom half of table 3-2 shows that reserve ratio multiples in all three sets of states fell sharply during the decade but that the relative rankings of the medians for the three groups were preserved. Nonborrowing states had a median multiple of 1.19 with 10 of 14 being above 1.0 and none below .5. Only 5 of the 10 with loans of $100 million or more in the 1970s had positive net reserves and not one of this group had a reserve ratio multiple as large as .5. As noted in chapter 1, only two state UI programs entered the 1980s with multiples above 1.5, the recommended minimum guideline for trust fund adequacy.[3]

Given the generally low levels of 1979 year-end reserve ratio multiples, the number of states requiring loans in the 1980-83 period is, in fact, quite low. Forty-nine states had multiples below 1.5 and 29 of them (59 percent) borrowed during this four-year period. Compared to the experience of the 1970s, this is a much lower proportion, i.e., 13 of 16 (81 percent) with multiples below 1.5 in 1969 borrowed in the 1972-79 period. The lower incidence of borrowing in 1980-83 among states with multiples below 1.5 occurred even though the initial distribution in the later period was concentrated more heavily at the lower reserve ratio multiples. Of the states with initial multiples in the 1.0-1.49 range, for example, 12 of 15 (80 percent) borrowed in the 1970s while only 1 of 11 (9 percent, Wisconsin) borrowed during 1980-83. This contrast in borrowing behavior strongly suggests that states have been more active in trying to avoid borrowing in the 1980s when compared to the 1970s.

To maintain adequate trust fund reserves it is important that employer taxes be increased after onset of a recession and the associated increase in UI benefit payments. Increases in flat rate taxes, proportional tax surcharges, increased taxes under pre-existing experience rating schedules and raising the taxable wage base per worker are the main ways of increasing effective tax rates. States where these changes occur quickly are less likely to encounter financing problems than states that respond slowly.

Tax increases in states where reserves are declining blunt the effectiveness of UI as an automatic stabilizer of economic activity. The need for tax increases points up the desirability of building adequate reserve balances in periods of prosperity. Because recessions have occurred with such frequency and severity since 1969, UI programs have not experienced the sustained periods of prosperity essential for rebuilding trust fund reserves. Until large enough reserves are re-established states will be required to raise taxes, reduce benefits and/or borrow during recessions as a direct consequence of their earlier as well as current inadequate reserve balances.

Table 3-3 presents summary information on changes in effective employer tax rates (based on total payrolls) following the major recession of the mid-1970s. The recessionary trough occurred in 1975 and the table shows the distribution of states by the percent changes in their average effective tax rates between 1975 and 1977.[4] For the entire U.S., the median percentage increase in tax rates was 51 percent. Eleven states raised effective tax rates by more than 100 percent and 31 by at least 40 percent. Among the 10 states with the largest loans in the 1970s, the median increase was only 20 percent and 3 increased effective tax rates by less than 10 percent. For the other two groups of states (the 14 that have never borrowed and the remaining 27) the median effective tax rate

increases were 40 and 63 percent respectively. Proportionately more states in these latter two categories made large tax
rate adjustments. The adjustments helped to prevent larger
debts from being incurred and hastened the pace of debt
repayment in the late 1970s.

Table 3-3
Distribution of States by Percentage Tax Rate Increases
Between 1975 and 1977; States Grouped by Borrowing Characteristics

Percent increase in average employer tax rate 1975-77[a]	Number of states by borrowing characteristics			
	All states	Did not borrow 1972-1983[b]	All other states[b]	Ten largest borrowers in 1970s[b]
Total	51	14	27	10
Negative	3	1	1	1
0-9.9	4	2	0	2
10-19.9	6	1	3	2
20-39.9	7	3	3	1
40-59.9	10	2	6	2
60-79.9	5	1	3	1
80-99.9	5	1	3	1
100-149.9	9	3	5	0
150 and above	2	0	2	0
Median percent increase[c]	51	40	63	20

SOURCE: Average tax rates based on data in U.S. Department of Labor, *Unemployment Insurance Financial Data* (1984).

a. Effective average tax rates measured as the ratio of total contributions to total covered wages. Tax rate increases refer to the 1975-77 period in forty-six states and to other periods in five states. The latter five were Connecticut (1971-77), Illinois (1973-77), New York (1975-79), Vermont (1973-77) and Washington (1971-77).

b. The identity of individual states within the three groups is indicated in footnote (a) of table 3-1 and column (1) of table 3-1. The ten largest borrowers are states that borrowed in excess of $100 million between 1972 and 1979.

c. Computer at The Urban Institute.

From tables 3-2 and 3-3, it is clear that the need for large
loans in the 1970s was associated with two factors: (i) low initial trust fund reserves and (ii) failure to enact major tax in-

creases following recessions. The 10 states with the largest loans in the 1970s had generally smaller than average reserve ratio multiples at the start of the decade and most made smaller than average tax rate changes following the onset of their financing problems. When they experienced high unemployment rates in the 1970s, they needed large loans to meet the demand for UI benefit payments.

Active Policies and Debt Avoidance

It is obvious that increasing effective tax rates and reducing benefit payments are the two ways to improve a UI program's solvency. Chapter 2 documented important solvency changes made in 10 major debtor states in the 1980s. The issue will be further explored here: first by examining the 10 states that borrowed the most in the 1970s and then by briefly discussing California and Florida, two states that have successfully avoided major debt problems.

Table 3-4 helps in summarizing active policies pursued in the 10 states requiring the largest loans in the 1970s. Item 1 shows total borrowing between 1972 and 1979. Combined, the 10 accounted for $5,074 million in loans or 91.1 percent of the national total for the period. The first loan year is shown in item 2 and for seven states it was 1975.

Key elements of active state policy to improve solvency are then identified in items 3 through 7. The time period covered by these items is from the first loan year (or just before that year) through 1980, i.e., a time period reflecting decisions made in the 1970s. High average tax rates based on taxable wages are noted in items 3 and 4. Seven states had average tax rates that exceeded 3 percent in at least three years and three had average rates of 4 percent or more in at least two years. These identify the states willing to levy high rates on employers. Illinois, Connecticut, and Minnesota are three states that did not apply such high tax rates following the onset of indebtedness.

Table 3-4
Ten States with the Largest Loans in the 1970s:[a]
Policy Actions and Loan Activity

	PA	IL	NJ	MI	CT	NY	MA	MN	WA	RI
(1) Total borrowed in the 1970s ($ millions)	1222	946	735	624	514	336	265	172	149	111
(2) Year of first loan	1975	1975	1975	1975	1972	1977	1975	1975	1973	1975
Average tax rate (based on taxable wages) after first loan[b]										
(3) Rate above 3 percent for 3 or more years	X					X	X		X	X
(4) Rate above 4 percent for 2 or more years			X	X			X			
Taxable wage base changes after first loan[b,c]										
(5) Temporary increase to above FUT taxable wage base					X					X
(6) Permanent increase to above FUT taxable wage base			X						X	
(7) Freeze on maximum weekly benefit amount after first loan				X		X		X		
(8) 1970s loans fully repaid				X		X				
(9) 1980-83 unemployment rate (percent)	9.7	9.9	7.8	13.6	6.2	8.1	6.7	6.8	10.2	8.3
(10) Major borrowing in the 1980-83 period[d]	X	X		X				X		

SOURCES: Items (2)-(6) based on U.S. Department of Labor, *Unemployment Insurance Financial Data* (1984). Item (7) based on U.S. Department of Labor, "Significant Provisions of State Unemployment Insurance Laws," various issues. Items (1), (8), (9), and (10) based on unpublished U.S. Labor Department data.

a. States which borrowed $100 million or more between 1972 and 1979.

b. Changes cover the period from the first loan year (or just before that year) through 1980.

c. Temporary increases in the taxable wage base are defined as increases which were subsequently matched or superseded by increases in the FUT taxable wage base. Permanent tax base increases refer to increases that kept the state's taxable wage base above the FUT taxable wage base.

d. Major borrowing in item (10) is defined as 1980-83 loans equal to at least 1 percent of 1979 total covered payrolls.

Six of the 10 states increased the taxable wage base per employee as a means for easing their financing problems. Defining as temporary a tax base increase to above the FUT taxable wage base if it remained above the federal base that applied for just a limited number of years, there were temporary increases in three states (Michigan to $5,400 in 1976-77, Connecticut to $6,000 in 1975-77, and Rhode Island to $4,800 in 1975-77). Three permanent increases in state taxable wage bases, i.e., bases that remained above the FUT taxable base, were also instituted. New Jersey raised its maximum to $4,800 in 1975 and indexed it to the average weekly wage starting in 1976. Minnesota's maximum that already had been $4,800 since 1966 was raised to $6,200 in 1976, $7,000 in 1977 and $8,000 in 1979. Finally, Washington, in anticipation of funding problems, instituted a type of tax base indexing in 1971 that has been followed in subsequent years. Four of these debtor states (Pennsylvania, Illinois, New York and Massachusetts) did nothing active to their taxable wage bases except to match the federal base increase from $4,200 in 1977 to $6,000 in 1978.[5]

One comparatively simple way to conserve on benefit payments is to freeze the maximum weekly benefit amount. Michigan and New York did not have indexed maximums in the 1970s and thus could easily restrict the growth in weekly benefits by not legislating new higher maximums. Michigan's maximum for a single beneficiary was maintained at $97 between 1975 and February 1981. New York kept its maximum at $95 between 1974 and 1977 and then at $125 between 1979 and 1983. In both states the average weekly benefit payment as a proportion of the average weekly wage in covered employment declined noticeably while the benefit maximums were held constant.[6] In the other eight states, maximum benefit amounts continued to rise.

The data summarized in items 3-7 suggest a variety of responses by the 10 states to their financing problems of the

1970s. At one extreme Illinois made none of the changes described in the table while Pennsylvania, Connecticut and Minnesota made only one of the indicated changes. Policy changes were most obvious in Michigan but at least two of the three steps (high tax rates, tax base increases and a freeze on maximum benefits) were also taken in New Jersey, New York, Washington and Rhode Island.

There is some, albeit imperfect, association between the indicated state policy actions and two important financing conditions identified in items 8 and 10 of table 3-4—full repayment of loans from the 1970s and the need for major borrowing in the 1980s.[7] Among the four states with less active policy responses, three have not paid off their loans from the 1970s (Pennsylvania, Illinois, and Connecticut) and three (Pennsylvania, Illinois, and Minnesota) have been major borrowers in the 1980-83 period. Among the five described as most active in making changes, three have paid off their loans from the 1970s (Michigan, New York, and Washington) while only one (Michigan) has been a major borrower during 1980-83. Other factors such as unemployment rates (item 9) and subsequent UI legislation also have effects on these two financial outcomes. From table 3-4, however, it seems clear that active state legislative responses have aided in both repaying the loans from the 1970s and avoiding the need for large additional loans in the 1980s.

At the end of 1983 four state UI programs had trust fund balances that exceeded $500 million. The states and their balances were as follows; California-$2,169 million, New York-$961 million, Florida-$888 million and Massachusetts-$532 million. Three of the four (all but California) required federal UI loans in the 1970s, but all three repaid these advances quite promptly. Massachusetts was in debt for the longest period, borrowing first in 1975 and completing its repayments in 1980. Having quite large trust fund balances in 1983, at the end of a prolonged recessionary period, reflects the effects of earlier state policy actions. Massachusetts subjected its employers to very high average tax rates in the late 1970s. This coupled with relatively low unemployment in the 1980s (observe in table 3-4 the average 1980-83 rate was 6.7 percent while the national average was 8.5 percent) resulted in a major accumulation of trust fund balances after 1977.[8] It has already been noted (table 3-4) that New York also imposed high tax rates in the late 1970s and sharply limited the growth in maximum weekly benefits between 1974 and 1983. The recent histories of the California and Florida programs deserve more extensive comments because they both illustrate how an active policy response can prevent the emergence of a serious UI funding problem.

California has a long history of vigorous policy actions to ensure UI program solvency. It maintained a high taxable wage base, i.e., one that exceeded the FUT taxable wage base, continuously between 1960 and 1971. When trust fund balances were reduced in the 1958 and 1960-61 recessions, large tax rate increases occurred in 1959 and again in 1962. Strong policy actions also helped to maintain the trust fund in the 1970s, a decade when the state experienced unusually high unemployment.

Appendix table A11 presents summary data on trust fund balances, benefits and UI taxes in California since 1970. Between 1970 and 1979, the state's unemployment rate averaged 7.9 percent (1.7 percentage points above the national average), and the state's rate exceeded the national unemployment rate in each of these 10 years. The table shows that compared to the national average the California program compensates a similar proportion of its unemployed and that its average weekly benefits replace a slightly smaller proportion of its average weekly wages (columns 10 and 11 respectively). Due to California's high unemployment, annual benefit outlays averaged 1.38 percent of total payrolls in the 1970s, a payout rate that was 20 percent higher than the national average of 1.15 percent.

California entered the 1970s with a trust fund balance of $1,305 million and a reserve ratio multiple of 1.43 (columns 1 and 2 of table A11). After the 1970-71 recession reduced reserves by about $400 million, a substantial increase in average tax rates levied on taxable wages (from 2.19 percent in 1971 to 2.72 and 3.01 percent in the next two years) helped restore the trust fund balance to $1,221 million at the start of 1974. The next increased demand for benefits occurred in 1974-75, causing the balance to be reduced to $546 million and the reserve ratio multiple fell to .38 by the start of 1976.

A set of policy actions fully effective in 1976 and 1977 again helped restore the state's trust fund balance. (1) The taxable wage base was raised from $4,200 to $7,000 in 1976-77. (2) Tax rates applied to taxable wages generally rose during 1976-79, as the result of the state's experience rated tax rate structure within a range of from 1.4 to 4.9 percent.[9] (3) The weekly benefit maximum was not raised above its 1976 level of $104 until 1980. As a consequence, average weekly benefits as a proportion of average weekly wages declined from .335 in 1976 (already below the national average) to .292 in 1979. Due to these policy decisions and the response of experience rated taxes, the state's trust fund balance was restored to $2,738 million by the start of 1980. This level represented about 32 percent of total net reserves for all 51 UI programs in the U.S. at that time. Although the reserve balance has not grown much since 1980, neither has it fallen despite the recessions.[10]

To illustrate the scale of discretionary policy actions from the 1970s, it is useful to note the revenue effects due to raising the taxable wage base to $7,000 in 1976 and 1977. The higher tax base increased taxable wages by about $11.6 and $13.8 billion in these two years respectively.[11] Applying average tax rates from 1976 and 1977 (column 15 of table A11) to these taxable wage increments yields a two-year estimated increase in total revenues of about $850 million. Subtracting these estimated revenues from the trust fund balance at the start of 1980 reduces it from $2.7 billion to $1.9 billion. The end of 1983 balance would be $1.3 billion rather than $2.2 billion if not for the added revenues from the 1976-77 tax base increase. Thus, a large trust fund balance in the 1980s is the direct consequence of large scale policy actions taken during the 1970s. California was able to pass through the 1980-83 period without further large scale changes in its UI taxes and/or benefits because of the tax base increases and other active policies consistently implemented in the 1970s and earlier.

Florida's history also illustrates how strong policy actions can restore a trust fund balance in a relatively short time period. Traditionally, Florida has had a UI program characterized by low taxes and low benefits. Between 1947 and 1969, benefits exceeded 1 percent of payroll in just two years (1949 and 1962) while taxes equalled or exceeded 1 percent of total payrolls in just three years (1947, 1961, and 1962). Florida entered the 1970s with a trust fund balance of $256 million and a reserve ratio multiple of 2.42 (see table A12). A situation of low taxes and low benefits persisted in the first half of the 1970s as well. Table A12 shows that low benefit costs in Florida are partly due to compensating a low fraction of the unemployed (column 10) and paying relatively low weekly benefits (column 11).

The recession of 1974-75 was especially severe in Florida. The state's unemployment rate exceeded the national average in every year between 1974 and 1979 (column 9). Employment dropped sharply in construction and in several other industries causing UI claims to be particularly heavy in 1975. Because payouts were so large in 1975, the trust fund balance fell from $326 million at the start of the year to $80 million 12 months later. Over this same period the state's reserve ratio multiple fell from 1.51 to .23, one of the largest declines ever experienced by a state UI program during a one-year period. Small loans were obtained in both 1975 and 1976 to ensure that the state had adequate reserves to make its benefit payments.

Florida's policy response to this situation was immediate and vigorous. Average tax rates on taxable wages nearly doubled between 1975 and 1976 (column 15) and they averaged above 2.5 percent in the next two years.[12] The weekly benefit maximum was not raised above its 1975 level of $82 over the next three years and then was set at $95 in 1979 and 1980. As a result the average benefit-wage ratio declined from .358 in 1975 to .319 in 1978 and then to .311 in 1980.

As benefit claims declined to more normal levels in the late 1970s, the effects of these policy actions on the trust fund became apparent. The balance grew from $24 million at the start of 1977 to $665 million three years later. Like California, Florida entered the 1980s with a net trust fund balance more than twice as large as 10 years earlier. Although neither state achieved a reserve ratio multiple of 1.5, reserves have been adequate to meet all benefit payments in the 1980s without the need for federal UI loans or sharp increases in employer tax rates.

It should be noted that each of the four states with the largest trust fund balances at the end of 1983 experienced average or below average unemployment in the 1980-83 period.[13] Furthermore, in both California and Florida rapid growth in the state's economy has also helped to maintain large reserves (see section on Economic Growth and Trust Fund Balances). Even with active policies and good experiences with uncontrollable factors such as unemployment and economic growth, not one of these states had a reserve ratio multiple as large as 1.0 at the end of 1983, much less the 1.5 multiple often used as a guideline for judging fund adequacy. If economic growth remains strong through the end of 1985, a 1.5 multiple is still not likely to be attained in any of the four states. This situation helps to illustrate the widespread loss of trust fund reserve adequacy that UI programs have recently experienced. Even the states with the largest reserve balances have low reserve ratio multiples.

From the examples of California and Florida as well as the experiences of the states needing large-scale loans in the 1970s, the efficacy of state policy actions is apparent. In states where declining reserve balances have triggered fast responses of tax increases and/or benefit reductions (more precisely benefit freezes), debts and large-scale borrowing have been avoided. Even after large-scale borrowing has occurred, strong policy actions have hastened the repayment of debts and helped to prevent renewed borrowing.

Tax Base Indexing

In chapter 1 it was noted that most state programs have indexed their maximum weekly benefit amount to the state average weekly wage but have not similarly indexed their taxable wage base. With the advent of higher inflation during the 1970s (recall table 1-4), many social programs and private sector wage contracts adopted indexation provisions. The social security (OASDHI) program, for example, has had a fully indexed taxable wage base since 1975. It requires an active policy decision to implement indexation, but once in place, indexation causes a program to make certain automatic adjustments in an inflationary environment. In the past, UI programs have exhibited an ambivalent attitude towards indexation. Although the maximum weekly benefit amount has been indexed in most states, there has been a reluctance to index the taxable wage base. The failure of the taxable wage base to rise automatically with inflation has contributed to UI financing problems in several states. This section examines the experience of states that have had indexed taxable wage bases for measurable periods of time.

Table 3-5 identifies 14 states that have tax base indexing provisions in their UI programs as of 1984.[14] In nine, the 1984 taxable wage base (column 1) exceeded $10,000 and in four the base fell between $9,600 and $10,000. Although high tax bases could be achieved by periodic legislated increases, it is interesting to note that only 9 of the 51 state tax bases exceeded $10,000 in 1984, and all nine were in states with indexed taxable wage bases. Among the states that have legislated their tax bases to exceed $7,000 (the FUT tax base since 1983) but have not indexed them, the highest 1984 tax bases were $9,600 in Wyoming and $9,500 in Wisconsin. Thus, in fact, the highest taxable wage bases are found in states with indexed wage bases.

Twelve of the states identified in table 3-5 (all but Montana and Washington) have what can be termed fully indexed wage bases. The UI laws in these states specify that the tax base is to be a certain percent of state average annual wage in covered employment. Thus the percentage increase in the annual taxable wage base equals the percentage increase in average annual wage from a preceding calendar or fiscal year. In Montana, the base is to be 75 percent of average annual wages but yearly increases are capped at $200. Washington's base is to equal 80 percent of average annual wages, but $600 annual increments automatically occur whenever the trust fund balance falls below 4.5 percent of total covered wages. Since 1971, these $600 increments have been implemented in each year.[15] Thus Montana and Washington can be described as having partially indexed UI tax bases. Under full indexation the 1984 tax bases in Montana and Washington would be $10,800 and $14,000 respectively, rather than $8,400 and $12,000 as shown in table 3-5.

Table 3-5
States with Indexed Taxable Wage Bases, 1984

State	Taxable wage base in 1984[a] (1)	First year of tax base indexation[b] (2)	Indexation timing and percentage		Ratio of taxable to total payrolls (for periods in column 3)[d]	
			Period of indexation (through 1982)[c] (3)	Indexation percentage of state average annual wage (4)	State (5)	U.S. average (6)
Alaska	21,400[a]	1981	1981-82	60[a]	.491	.414
Hawaii	14,600	1965	1965-76[c]	90	.683	.500
			1977-82[c]	100	.693	.449
Idaho	14,400	1976	1976-82	100	.686	.452
Iowa	10,400	1978	1978-82	66.7	.508	.449
Minnesota	9,800	1982	1982	60	.461	.405
Montana[e]	8,400[e]	1979	1979-82	75[e]	.623	.437
Nevada	10,700	1975	1975-82	66.7	.591	.452
New Jersey	9,600	1976	1976-82	53.8	.458	.452
New Mexico	9,800	1978	1978-82	65	.547	.449
North Dakota	10,400	1979	1979-82	70	.558	.437
Oregon	13,000	1976	1976-82	80	.603	.452
Rhode Island	10,000	1980	1980-82	70	.547	.425
Utah[f]	f	1977	1977-82	100[f]	.654	.449
Washington[g]	12,000[g]	1971	1971-82	80[g]	.570	.463

SOURCE: Data in columns (5) and (6) based on U.S. Department of Labor, *Unemployment Insurance Financial Data* (1984). Data in columns (1), (2), (3) and (4) based on U.S. Department of Labor, "Comparison of State Unemployment Insurance Laws," various issues.

a. Reflects indexation percentage shown in column (4) for 1982, except for Alaska where this percentage changed from 60 to 75 percent after 1982.

b. This column identifies the first year when the state's taxable wage base increased automatically to maintain a specified percentage of the state's average annual wage in covered employment.

c. Two periods indicated for Hawaii when different indexation percentages applied.

d. Ratios are simple averages of state ratios and U.S. ratios, in columns (5) and (6), respectively, for the years indicated in column (3). Each state ratio represents state taxable payrolls divided by total covered payrolls in the state. Each U.S. ratio represents the sum of all state taxable payrolls in all states divided by the national aggregate of total covered payrolls.

e. Although Montana's taxable wage base is indexed to 75 percent of the state's average annual wage, annual increases are limited to a maximum of $200. Thus the 1984 wage base was $8,400 rather than $10,800.

f. Utah's taxable wage base was frozen at the $12,000 level from 1981 through 1983 and then set at $13,300 for 1984 by legislation which also reduced the indexation percentage to 75 percent starting in 1985; the 1985 taxable wage base is $12,100.

g. Washington's taxable wage base is indexed at 80 percent of its average annual wage, but annual increments are to be $600 whenever the state's trust fund falls below 4.5 percent of total payrolls. This latter provision has prevailed since 1971 causing the 1984 maximum to be $12,000 rather than $14,000.

Tax base indexation is clearly a phenomenon of western states. Of the 14 states identified in the table, 4 are in the Pacific division (Alaska, Hawaii, Oregon and Washington), 5 are in the Mountain division (Idaho, Montana, Nevada, New Mexico, and Utah) and 3 are in the West North Central division (Iowa, Minnesota, and North Dakota). The only two states east of the Mississippi River with indexed bases are New Jersey and Rhode Island.

Indexing was instituted quite recently in most of these states. In some, indexing has been implemented following a period of discretionary tax base increases. In Alaska, for example, the tax base has exceeded the FUT tax base in every year since 1955 but indexation (where the tax base rises proportionately with the increase in average wages) was instituted only in 1981. Of the 14 states, 9 instituted indexation between 1976 and 1980 (column 2) while 2 did it in 1981-82. Thus the adoption of indexation appears to be due at least partially to the recession of the mid-1970s and a recognition of the need to enhance UI program revenues.

Indexation formulas are quite similar across the 14 states. The taxable wage base varies from 53.8 percent of the prior average annual wage in New Jersey up to 100 percent in Hawaii and Idaho (and in Utah between 1977 and 1981). Column 4 shows these percentages. They are applied to average annual wages in covered employment in the state for an earlier 12-month base period.[16] The base period is one, one-and-one-half, or two years prior to the current calendar year to which the tax base applies. In each state the taxable wage base, so computed, moves upward directly in response to the wage inflation experienced by that state.

Columns 5 and 6 of table 3-5 show the impact of indexation by comparing average ratios of taxable-to-total payrolls in each state to the average ratio for the entire U.S. These ratios are based on years through 1982 (with the exact years identified in column 3), the latest year for which there are published data on taxable wages from all states. Among the 14 states where tax base indexation was in effect, the column 5 ratio is uniformly the higher of the two.[17] It is at least 40 percent higher than the column 6 average in three states (Hawaii, Idaho and Utah) where the tax base was 100 percent of the state's average annual wage, and in Montana where it was indexed at 75 percent. The state average ratio was between 20 and 39 percent higher in six states and less than 20 percent higher in four states. From the data for Hawaii, Idaho, and Utah in column 5, it appears that 66 to 70 percent of covered wages are taxable when the taxable wage base is set at 100 percent of the state's average annual wage.

Hawaii has experienced the longest continuous period of wage indexation, covering the period from 1965 to the present. A closer examination of this period is useful for illustrating how the ratio of taxable-to-total payrolls depends on the inflation rate as well as the percentage of the state's average annual wage to which the taxable wage base is tied. Prior to 1977, the tax base in Hawaii was set at 90 percent of the average annual wage for the 12 months ending on June 30 of the previous year. Because inflation was much lower in the 1960s than in the 1970s, the state's taxable-to-total payrolls ratio fell a little from .694 to .675 between 1965-69 and 1970-76. After the tax base was raised from 90 to 100 percent of the average annual wage in 1977, the average taxable-to-total ratio then increased to .693 in the 1977-82 period. Due to the continued high inflation of the 1977-82 period, however, the average ratio was not higher than in 1965-69, despite the increase in the index percentage (from 90 to 100) to which the taxable wage base was indexed. These data from Hawaii show that higher inflation does cause the taxable-to-total ratio to decline, but this decline is a much less serious problem than the erosion in the ratio that occurs when the taxable wage base is not indexed.[18]

Although tax base indexation has not been tried for prolonged periods in many states, an analysis of their financing problems in the 1970s and 1980s can be instructive. Table 3-6 identifies the 10 states whose taxable wage bases have been continuously above the FUT taxable wage base for the longest periods, including years of discretionary increases prior to indexation in a few states. The first year of the continuously higher tax base is shown in column 1. In three (Alaska, Hawaii and Minnesota), this year preceded 1970 while in five it occurred in either 1975 or 1976. Nine of the ten (all but Idaho) have had to borrow from the federal UI loan fund at some point in their history. In five (Alaska, Washington, Oregon, Nevada and New Jersey) the higher wage base was instituted at about the time they first borrowed while in the other five (Hawaii, Minnesota, Idaho, Iowa and Utah) the imposition of a higher tax base occurred at least five years prior to the year of their first loan. Even among the latter group, however, a perception that trust fund balances were unacceptably low was one reason why their taxable wage bases were raised. Four of the five (all but Hawaii) had reserve ratio multiples below 1.5 at the start of the period of permanently higher wage bases.[19] It seems clear that a perceived financing problem existed in nine of the ten states at the time their wage bases were permanently raised. Higher tax bases were desired to help pay off existing debts, to reduce current deficits and to prevent future indebtedness.

Columns 3 and 4 then identify other actions taken by these states to enhance UI program revenues in the 1970s. Six of the ten enacted at least one more increase in their taxable wage base to a level above what was contemplated when the permanently higher taxable wage base (column 1) was first implemented. Indexing was introduced in Oregon (1976), Iowa (1978) and Utah (1977) while the indexing percentage was raised in Hawaii (1977). Further discretionary tax base increases were implemented in Alaska (1974) and Minnesota

Table 3-6
Policy Actions and Borrowing Activities in Ten States
with the Longest Histories of Consistently High Taxable Wage Bases

State	First year state tax base continuously above FUT tax base (1)	Year of first loan (2)	Years actions taken after 1970 to raise the trust fund balance		Average tax rate (as percent of total wages) 1977-79 (5)	Major borrowing in the 1970s (6)	Average unemployment rate in 1980-83 (percent) (7)	Major borrowing in the 1980-83 period (8)
			Further tax base increase (3)	Major tax rate increase (4)				
Alaska	1955	1955	1974, 1981, 1983	1976	2.57	NA	9.8	NA
Hawaii	1962	1975	1977	1972, 1975, 1977	2.23	NO	5.9	NO
Minnesota	1966	1975	1976-1978, 1982	1977	1.25	YES	6.8	YES
Washington	1971	1973	NO	1972, 1978	1.80	YES	10.2	NO
Oregon	1974	1976	1976	1976	2.06	NO	10.1	NO
Nevada	1975	1976	NO	1972, 1976	1.80	NO	8.3	NO
New Jersey	1975	1975	NO	1973	1.93	YES	7.8	NO
Idaho	1976	NA	NO	1977, 1984	1.47	NA	8.8	NA
Iowa	1976	1982	1978, 1985	1976, 1984	1.38	NA	7.3	YES
Utah	1976	1982	1977	1983	1.16	NA	7.5	NO

SOURCE: Data in columns (1), (2) and (5) based on U.S. Department of Labor, *Unemployment Insurance Financial Data*, (1984). Columns (3) and (4) based on U.S. Department of Labor, "Significant Provisions of State Unemployment Insurance Laws," various issues, and the author's judgment. Columns (2), (6), (7) and (8) based on unpublished U.S. Labor Department data. Major borrowing in columns (6) and (8) defined as loans totaling at least one percent of total payroll (in 1975 and 1979 respectively).

NA = Not applicable as the state did not borrow.

(1976-78). Increases in the state's tax rate schedule, i.e., increases in the tax schedule that affected both the minimum and maximum tax rates, occurred at least once in all 10 states during the 1970s. Thus higher average tax rates and further tax base increases were common in the states that already had a taxable wage base higher than the FUT taxable wage base. In summary, all of these states took two or more policy actions to substantially increase program revenues in the 1970s and the dates of these actions are shown in columns 1, 3, and 4.

The effects of the policy actions on average effective tax rates are shown in column 5. During 1977-79 effective tax rates, as a percentage of total wages, averaged 1.30 percent for the U.S. as a whole. Eight of these states (all but Minnesota and Utah) had tax rate averages that were higher than the national average, and in six the state average was more than 30 percent higher than the national average. The state policy actions generally resulted in quite high average tax rates.

Columns 6 and 8 then examine the borrowing activities of these states in the 1970s and 1980s. Presumably they would have less need to borrow as a consequence of raising their tax bases and tax rates. For both the 1972-79 and 1980-83 periods major borrowing by a state can be defined as a loan total that exceeds 1 percent of total wages. Recall from table 3-1 (columns 2 and 4) that 13 states required major loans in 1972-79 and 13 were major borrowers in 1980-83.[20] Three states identified in table 3-6 (Minnesota, New Jersey, and Washington) were major borrowers in the 1970s and two (Minnesota and Iowa) were major borrowers in the 1980-83 period.

It is interesting to speculate how much borrowing would have occurred if these states had not instituted higher taxable wage bases. To pursue this question, a rough calculation was made to estimate the effects of the higher tax bases on trust fund balances and the need for loans in the 1970s. Using historic data on total benefit payments and average employer tax rates (on taxable payrolls) it was estimated that Hawaii and Alaska would also have been major borrowers in the 1970s if their taxable wage bases had remained continuously at the level of the FUT taxable wage base between 1970 and 1979.[21] Higher taxable wage bases prevented these two states from needing major loans in the 1970s.[22] Higher tax bases reduced the need for loans in the three states that already were major borrowers. The calculations suggested that Minnesota, New Jersey, and Washington would have needed an additional $27, $54 and $160 million respectively.[23] Among the seven states that would have had to borrow at least once in the 1970s (all but Idaho, Iowa and Utah) the calculations showed that the higher tax bases reduced total loans by $307 million (from $1,399 to $1,092 million) or by more than 20 percent from what would have been borrowed between 1972 and 1979 had their tax bases remained at the level of the FUT tax base.

Only two of these ten states have been major borrowers in the 1980-83 period. Chapter 2 has already noted Minnesota's problems in devising acceptable UI solvency legislation in 1983 and 1984. Despite comparatively low unemployment rates, its recent legislative deadlock led to the emergence of a sizable debt in the early 1980s. Iowa's 1980-83 funding problem stems directly from a long period of unusually high demand for benefits. Between 1947 and 1974 the state did not have a single year when benefits were as high as 1 percent of total payrolls. In the eight years from 1975 to 1982, however, benefits exceeded 1 percent of payrolls in seven years and equaled .99 percent of payrolls in the eighth. The highest rate of payout occurred in 1982 (2.43 percent of payrolls) with 1980 and 1981 ranking second and fourth respectively of all years since 1947. A rough calculation suggested that the state's high tax base has increased total revenues by $109 million between 1976 and 1983 and that actual borrowing during 1980-83 ($324 million) would have been $72 million higher if not for these added revenues. Thus a long period of high payouts has caused a need for major loans even with an indexed tax base.[24] Finally, observe in columns 7 and 8 that Alaska, Washington and Oregon have avoided large-scale borrowing despite the fact that their unemployment rates in 1980-83 have been considerably higher than the national average of 8.5 percent. Avoiding the need for large loans in the face of very high unemployment is partly the result of tax base indexing.

A given amount of payroll tax revenue can be raised by various combinations of taxable wage bases and scheduled tax rates applied to taxable wages. Legislating higher tax bases could have effects on state tax rates. It has already been noted that the 10 high tax base states showed a willingness to increase their average tax rates in the 1970s (column 4 in table 3-6). There is evidence, however, that maximum tax rates may be affected by the presence of high taxable wage bases. By 1985 all states are required by federal law to have a maximum tax rate of at least 5.4 percent of taxable wages. In 1984, 19 of the 51 states had maximum rates below 5.4 percent. Six of the 19 are among the 10 states with permanently higher tax bases identified in table 3-6. Thus 6 of these 10 were required to raise their maximum tax rates in 1985 whereas only 13 of the 41 other states (or 32 percent) had to enact such increases. More than one factor may cause the maximum tax rate to be generally lower in states with higher taxable wage bases. Part of the reason for generally lower maximum tax rates in the 10 states, however, may be that indexation has helped these states to keep revenues more in balance with benefit payments over the long run.

Tax base indexing has been present in enough states for sufficiently long periods to draw certain conclusions about its efficacy. (1) Indexing has resulted in much higher taxable wage bases. As noted above, all nine states with taxable wage bases above $10,000 in 1984 were states with indexed tax bases. (2) Tax base indexing has had major effects on tax revenues in both the 1970s and 1980s. Without indexing, Hawaii and Alaska would have been major borrowers in the 1970s (total loans exceeding 1 percent of 1975 total wages) and required loans would have been much larger in Minnesota, New Jersey and Washington, states that already were major borrowers. States that had adopted tax base indexing by the mid-1970s required relatively smaller loans than the average for all other states in the 1980s. (3) Indexing has not eliminated the need for states to make other discretionary adjustments in trying to maintain program solvency. Iowa's problems in the 1980s vividly illustrate this point. Because indexing has tended to increase program revenues, however, it has reduced the size of other tax and benefit adjustments that states have needed to make. The borrowing of the 1970s and 1980s would undoubtedly have been much smaller if all states had entered the 1970s with fully indexed taxable wage bases. With indexed taxable wage bases, UI revenues would have maintained a better balance with benefit payments in the face of the high inflation rates of the 1970s and 1980s.

Tax base indexing is a discretionary policy action taken by certain states that has obvious positive long-run implications for UI program revenues. As noted in table 3-6, however, states with indexed tax bases have also instituted other active policies to produce a better balance between taxes and benefit payments. Conversely, states like California and Florida have instituted policy actions other than indexing to achieve the same solvency objective. Thus, tax base indexing by itself is neither necessary nor sufficient for maintaining program solvency. What it clearly has done, however, is reduce the scale of the UI fiscal imbalances that developed in several states both in the 1970s and in the 1980s.

Economic Growth and Trust Fund Balances

At the start of chapter 3 uncontrollable factors were identified that can affect a state's UI program solvency and borrowing needs: its current trust fund balance, unemployment and the rate of economic growth. The effects of low trust fund balances and high unemployment on borrowing needs are immediate and easily described. Economic growth also can have important effects but these effects are manifested more in the long run that in the short run. This section discusses the effects of economic growth on solvency.

Chapter 1 noted that a high rate of economic growth in a state has a positive effect on its UI trust fund balance. Because disparities in regional growth rates were especially pronounced in the 1970s, experiences from this decade are particularly relevant. Companies relocated away from so-called frost belt states of the North to places in the South and West in record numbers. The absence of a previous research literature on this topic will prevent the present discussion from reaching definitive conclusions. Given the topic's importance, however, an initial analysis is appropriate.

Institutional features of UI programs cause state trust fund balances to be affected in a differential manner when there are large-scale net flows of jobs and workers from one state to another. Benefits and taxes both respond differentially in origin and destination states when jobs and workers move. The net effect of geographic mobility is to raise the trust fund balance in destination states while lowering it in the states that workers leave. In the following paragraphs, these effects will be discussed from the perspective of a plant closure in one state accompanied by a plant opening in another state. Similar effects are also operative when employment levels of existing plants are reduced in one state but expanded elsewhere. The latter situations, in fact, probably affect more workers than plant closures and openings.

Four effects on the benefits side of UI programs are noteworthy. (1) In states losing jobs due to plant closures and relocations, the loss of job slots will tend to raise unemployment, especially long term unemployment, among older workers who are reluctant to move. Long term unemployment of older workers, i.e., 45 and over, will reduce UI trust fund balances because these workers are the ones most likely to collect UI benefits. (2) For laid-off workers who try to secure jobs in another state but are not successful, claims for benefits based on prior employment remain the financial responsibility of the UI program in the state where the plant closure occurred. (3) Workers who find jobs in states where new plants are opened must work for a minimum time period and earn a minimum amount of covered wages before qualifying for UI benefits. Those laid off before the qualifying requirements are achieved cannot draw benefits while others who just satisfy the qualifying requirements will not be eligible for maximum weekly benefits and maximum benefit duration. (4) States with numerous new plant openings are more likely to have conditions of strong labor demand and low unemployment. This will help to minimize the duration of insured unemployment and limit the payment of benefits to individual unemployed workers further conserving trust fund balances. In all four effects, there is either a loss to the trust fund of the origin state or a limit on benefit outlays from the destination state's trust fund.

Two effects on the revenue side of UI programs may also be important. (5) Plants that close represent an immediate loss of UI tax revenues. In origin states, claims for benefits may completely exhaust the trust fund balance for a firm whose plant has closed. The excessive claims will eventually result in ineffectively charged benefits that must be covered by taxes paid by the remaining employers in the state. (6) New employers typically pay a higher-than-average UI tax rate in their first two or three years of operation in order to build up their trust fund balances. In states where frequent plant openings are occurring, higher taxes on new employers could have an effect of raising the overall trust fund balance. As long as rapid growth continues to occur there will always be several new employers paying these higher taxes before they are eligible to be experience rated.

The direction of the effect on trust fund balances is clear in each of the six situations just described. What is crucial, but not known, is the aggregate importance of these separate factors that raise trust funds in destination states while lowering them in origin states.

Table 3-7 focuses on trust fund reserve ratio multiples in 1969 and 1979 controlling for employment growth during the 1970s. The states are stratified into three groups: the fastest growing 13, the next 25 and the slowest growing 13. To give an idea of the growth disparities, overall employment growth was 36.3 percent between 1969 and 1979. Idaho, the state with the 13th highest rate, grew 74.8 percent while Maryland, the state with the 13th lowest rate, grew by only 27.2 percent. On average, employment in the top 13 grew by 85.7 percent, more than six times the 13.7 average percent growth experienced by the bottom 13 during the 1970s.[25]

The most rapidly growing states entered the 1970s with higher than average reserve ratio multiples. Table 3-7 shows that while the median multiple for all 51 states was 1.84 at the end of 1969, these states had a median of 2.24. In contrast, the slowest growing states entered the 1970s with a median reserve ratio multiple of only 1.46.[26]

By the end of the 1970s reserve ratio multiples had declined in all states. Table 3-7 shows that states with the fastest employment growth were more successful at maintaining their reserves than were the others. While the national median multiple had declined to .63 (34 percent of its 1969 level), the median multiple for fastest growing states had declined to .90 (40 cent of its 1969 level). Five of the states with fastest growth had 1979 reserve ratio multiples of 1.0 or above while not one fell below .5. In contrast, the 1979 median for the 13 slowest growing states was –.07 and only two had multiples that exceeded .50.

Table 3-7
Distribution of States by Year and Reserve Ratio Multiples 1969 and 1979; States Grouped by Degree of 1969-1979 Employment Growth

Period and reserve ratio multiple	Number of states by degree of 1969-1979 employment growth[a]			
	All states	Fastest growing states	All other states	Slowest growing states
Total	51	13	25	13
End of 1969				
Negative	0	0	0	0
0-.49	0	0	0	0
.50-.99	1	0	0	1
1.00-1.49	15	3	6	6
1.50-1.99	14	2	7	5
2.00-2.99	13	6	7	0
3.00 and above	8	2	5	1
Median multiple[b]	1.84	2.24	1.96	1.46
End of 1979				
Negative	9	0	2	7
0-.49	12	0	8	4
.50-.99	17	8	7	2
1.00-1.49	11	5	6	0
1.50-1.99	2	0	2	0
2.00-2.99	0	0	0	0
3.00 and above	0	0	0	0
Median multiple[b]	.63	.90	.68	-.07

SOURCE: Based on data in U.S. Department of Labor, *Unemployment Insurance Financial Data* (1984).

a. Degree of growth based on the ratio of 1969 covered employment to 1979 covered employment. All the fastest growing states had an employment growth ratio of at least 1.748 while all the slowest growing states had an employment growth ratio below 1.273.

b. Computed at The Urban Institute.

Slow economic growth has a clear association with UI financing problems. Of the 13 states with the fastest employment growth, only two (Florida and Nevada) required any loans in the 1970s while four (Colorado, North Dakota, Texas and Utah) borrowed between 1980 and 1983.[27] Texas and Colorado have repaid their recent loans rather slowly. These two states, where 1980-83 loans exceeded 1 percent of 1979 total payrolls, can be described as major borrowers since 1980.[28]

Lending activity has been more common and much more substantial among the thirteen states with the slowest 1969-79 employment growth. Twelve borrowed sometime between 1972 and 1979 and nine had loans totaling at least 1 percent of 1975 total payrolls. In the 1980-83 period, ten of these same states have borrowed and for four (Illinois, Michigan, Ohio, and Pennsylvania) loans during 1980-83 totaled at least 4 percent of 1979 payrolls. Since seven of these slowest growing states entered the 1970s with reserve ratio multiples below 1.5 and seven entered the 1980s with negative reserve ratio multiples, it is hardly surprising that their ranks included so many large loan recipients in both periods. Given their low reserves at the end of 1979 it seems surprising that some have not needed even larger loans in the 1980s.

This chapter argued that initial trust fund balances were a major determinant of the need for federal UI loans in the 1970s. This same point is reemphasized by the data in table 3-7 and the discussion just completed. The latter discussion, however, has stressed that economic growth is also a determinant of trust fund balances and, hence, of the need for loans. States with high balances have achieved those balances not only through active policies but also through the effects of high growth, a factor largely beyond their own control.

As noted above, serious research has not yet addressed and provided estimates of how much rapid growth affects UI trust fund balances. One approach to this research question would be to develop a simulation model with two states (one fast growing and one slow growing) that have similar UI programs but different rates of birth and death of firms in covered employment, different rates of unemployment occurrences, different average unemployment durations and a net flow of workers from the slow growing to the fast growing state. One could insert realistic parameters describing UI taxes and benefits within such a simulation framework and isolate the effects of differential growth on trust fund balances in the two states. This type of research could eventually provide a basis for estimating how much the fastest growing states in the South and West have benefited from the recent increases in regional growth disparities.

Until the effect of differing growth rates on UI trust fund balances has been isolated, certain seemingly straightforward policy recommendations for restoring fiscal balance must be treated with caution. It will not help a debtor state much in the long run to raise employer taxes if that action intended to improve UI fund solvency also encourages employers to move their plants to other states. If faster growth confers major fiscal advantages to certain state UI programs, knowledge about the size of such effects would provide a basis for reinsurance and/or cost-sharing proposals to help states where low growth and high unemployment are concentrated. It is sufficient to end here by noting that growth disparities have been especially wide since 1970 and that financial advantages (of unknown size) have accrued to the UI programs in the fastest growing states.

Summary

This chapter has examined the issue of debt avoidance. One or more of the following conditions are present in states that have not required large scale UI loans since 1972: (i) large initial trust fund balances, (ii) willingness to implement active policies that raise revenues and reduce benefit payments when trust fund balances decline, (iii) having an indexed taxable wage base for UI payroll taxes, (iv) experiencing a low rate of unemployment, and (v) experiencing a rapid rate of economic growth. The second and third items in this list are things that individual states can control in the short run. Both can be viewed as active states responses to UI funding problems, since state legislative action is required to institute tax base indexing as well as to raise tax rate schedules and reduce benefit provisions. Once in place, an indexed tax base aids in keeping the revenue and benefit sides of a UI program in balance.

That active policy responses can lead to debt avoidance is hardly surprising. From the experiences of states that adopted tax base indexing, it is also clear that such indexing has reduced the scale but has not eliminated the need for discretionary tax and benefit changes when stagflation is present. States that act in a timely manner can avoid major funding problems.

Given the general deterioration in state UI trust fund balances that has occurred since 1969 (recall tables 1-2 and 3-2) it is also clear that states now must act more quickly in recessions than they ever had to in the past if they are to avoid borrowing. A second spur to faster state actions is the increased costs of loans and indebtedness in the 1980s compared to earlier periods. With smaller trust fund cushions and more expensive loan conditions, state UI is becoming more of a pay-as-you-go program as opposed to an automatic stabilizer. Pursuing more active policies also means that UI programs are becoming more willing to reduce benefits for the unemployed during the middle and later stages of recessions.

In contrast to the UI policy actions that the individual states control, the rate of economic growth and the unemployment rate are beyond state control. Rapid growth helps trust fund balances while slow growth has negative trust fund effects. Although the direction of the economic growth effect on trust fund balances is known, its size is not. As indicated above, this important topic should be pursued by further research. Many deficit states are in areas of slow growth but we do not currently know how much the slow growth has adversely affected their trust funds. The effects of high unemployment on trust fund balances are obvious and were examined in chapters 1 and 2.

Although rapid growth automatically helps a state's trust fund balance, it also seems that states in rapidly growing areas are more willing to use active policies to avoid UI trust fund debts. States in the West have pioneered in indexing the UI taxable wage base. They also have demonstrated a strong willingness to raise UI tax rates. Rapid growth may be linked to a state's willingness to act decisively to avoid deficits. If employers and workers, through their mobility, have already demonstrated a preference for residing in your state, they may be more willing to accept the consequences of the UI policy actions, e.g., higher employer taxes and lower benefits, needed to avoid trust fund indebtedness. As a broad generalization, this would seem to apply to states in the West more so than to states in the South. Reluctance of midwestern states to raise employer taxes could partly reflect a realistic concern to prevent even more employers, jobs and workers from moving to sun belt states. Thus rapid economic growth may both reduce the need for policy actions (because it helps in maintaining trust fund balances) and assist a state in taking the actions necessary to avoid debts (by reducing concerns about out migration of employers, jobs and workers).

NOTES

1. Besides the 37 states identified in table 3-1, one other state (Wyoming) borrowed for the first time in 1984. Washington, which had borrowed in the 1970s but not in 1980-83, also borrowed in 1984. Washington and Wyoming have already repaid their 1984 loans. Thus, a total of 31 states borrowed between 1980 and 1984 while 38 borrowed between 1972 and 1984.

2. Note that in nine of these ten states, 1972-79 loans also exceeded 1 percent of 1975 payrolls. Except for New York, large absolute loan amounts during 1972-79 also implied large relative loans as well. Because large absolute and relative loans cover so many of the same states, statements to be made about data in tables 3-2–3-4 (based on the 10 with loans in excess of $100 million) would also hold if large borrowers were defined by relative rather than absolute loan amounts.

3. For the 10 large debtor states examined in chapter 2, three (Pennsylvania, Illinois and New Jersey) had negative reserve ratio multiples at the end of 1979, four (Michigan, Ohio, Minnesota, and West Virginia) had multiples between 0 and .49, two (Texas and Louisiana) had multiples between .5 and .99 and one (Wisconsin) had a multiple between 1.0 and 1.49.

4. In five states, the percentage increases in effective average tax rates cover somewhat different time periods. In Connecticut, Vermont and Washington, the three states that needed loans before 1975, the periods were respectively 1971-77, 1973-77 and 1971-77. Because Illinois lowered its tax rate in 1975 the change was from 1973-74 (the two-year average) to 1977. The change in New York covered the period 1975-79 to give a two-year period following its first loan of 1977.

5. The FUT taxable wage base was increased to $6,000 in 1978, and all state UI programs in effect are required to have a taxable wage base at least equal to the FUT base.

6. In Michigan the average weekly benefit as a proportion of the average wage declined from .372 in 1975 to .316 in 1980. The ratio in New York declined from .339 in 1975 to .279 in 1982.

7. Major borrowing in the 1980s is defined as 1980-81 loans equal to at least 1 percent of 1979 total covered wages.

8. Net reserves were –$159 million at the start of 1978 and they increased by at least $100 million in each of the next four years.

9. The tax rate range was slightly lower, from 1.3 to 4.8 percent, in 1979.

10. The net reserve balance at the end of September 1984 was $2,854 million, about $100 million above its level of January 1, 1980.

11. This estimate was made at The Urban Institute. Using California data from other years its was estimated that taxable wages would have been .400 and .380 of total wages in 1976 and 1977 if the taxable wage base had remained at $4,200.

12. The minimum employer tax rate for the years 1975 to 1978 was .1, .7, 1.1 and 1.1 percent respectively. The maximum rate remained at 4.5 percent throughout the decade.

13. The U.S. unemployment rate averaged 8.5 percent for the four-year 1980-83 period. For the same four years the average unemployment rates in the four states were as follows: California 8.4 percent, Florida 7.4 percent, Massachusetts 6.7 percent and New York 8.1 percent.

14. Additionally North Carolina has a taxable wage base that is indexed to average taxable wages. Since the average taxable wage does not necessarily rise as general wage levels rise, this will not be considered an indexed wage base in the present discussion.

15. The tax base did not rise in 1974 but then it increased by $1,200 in 1975.

16. In New Jersey the tax base is designated to be 28 times the average weekly wage which is equivalent to 53.8 percent of average annual wages in covered employment.

17. Despite limitations on full indexation in Montana and Washington, and the freezing of the tax base in 1981 and 1982 in Utah, the ratios in these states exceeded the U.S. average ratios by substantial margins.

18. For example between 1965 and 1970 the annual taxable-to-total ratio in Hawaii declined from .708 to .680 or by 4.0 percent. For the overall U.S. during the same period the ratio declined from .558 to .447 or by 19.9 percent. A similar pattern is observed in 1978-82 when the FUT taxable wage base remained at $6,000. Hawaii's ratio barely changed from .697 in 1978 to .696 in 1982 while the national ratio declined from .496 to .405.

19. Reserve ratio multiples at the start of these periods were as follows: Hawaii (1962) 1.92; Minnesota (1966) .64; Idaho (1976) 1.23; Iowa (1976) .63 and Utah (1976) .71. The low multiples in Minnesota, Idaho, Iowa and Utah show these states had low reserves at the time their higher wage bases were adopted.

20. Recall from table 3-1 that loans in 1972-79 were measured relative to 1975 covered payrolls while 1980-83 loans were measured relative to 1979 payrolls.

21. The calculations started with the initial trust fund balances of January 1, 1970 and used estimates of interest income based on average yields for each year in the 1970s. With lower taxable wage bases it was estimated that Hawaii would have needed to borrow $61 million or 2.6 percent of 1975 total payrolls. Alaska would have needed $32 million or 1.3 percent of 1975 payrolls. All of these calculations were made at The Urban Institute.

22. Alternatively, these states could have further increased their tax rates (on taxable wages) and/or reduced benefit payments by freezing maximum weekly benefits in order to avoid the need for major loans. The point of the calculations was more to show the revenue and trust fund implications of instituting higher tax bases than to provide realistic counterfactual simulations of how finances would have evolved under a regime of lower tax bases.

23. The calculations shows even larger effects on total 1970-79 tax receipts and net trust fund balances at the end of 1979. Total tax receipts in Minnesota, New Jersey, and Washington were increased by $165 million, $196 million, and $357 million respectively, while 1979 net trust fund balances were raised by $182 million, $282 million, and $403 million respectively. The higher taxes allowed both Minnesota and Washington to end the decade of the 1970s with positive trust fund balances.

24. To further increase program revenues Iowa will raise its taxable wage base by an additional $1,100 and $1,600 in 1985 and 1986 respectively.

25. The 13 states with the highest growth rates were Alaska, Arizona, Colorado, Florida, Idaho, Nevada, New Mexico, North Dakota, Oklahoma, South Dakota, Texas, Utah and Wyoming. Two were from the North Central region, three from the South and eight from the West. The 13 with the slowest growth were Connecticut, Delaware, the District of Columbia, Illinois, Indiana, Maryland, Massachusetts, Michigan,

New Jersey, New York, Ohio, Pennsylvania and Rhode Island. Six of these states are from the North East region, four from the North Central region, and three from the South.

26. The fact that the fastest growing states entered the 1970s with above-average reserve ratio multiples is partly a reflection of high growth experienced by these states in earlier periods. For example, the 13 states that grew fastest in the 1970s experienced a total employment growth of 48.1 percent between 1959 and 1969. This growth rate was considerably higher than the national average (31.4 percent) and more than twice the 23.1 percent 1959-69 employment growth experienced by the 13 slowest growing states from the 1970s. A similar situation prevailed in the 1948-59 employment growth of 61.2 percent compared to national growth of 19.5 percent and growth of only 7.9 percent for the 13 slowest growing states (from the 1970s).

27. Wyoming which is also one of this group of states did borrow in 1984.

28. As noted in table 2-1 of chapter 2, however, the relative size of the Texas debt at the end of 1983 was much smaller than the relative debt size in the four states with the largest debts (Pennsylvania, Illinois, Michigan and Ohio). It might also be noted that energy production is important in Colorado as well as Texas. Recent borrowing by both states is partly due to the falloff in energy production after 1980.

4
Conclusions

The high demand for UI benefit payments since 1969 has created financing problems of differing severity for most state UI programs. Repeated and severe recessions have been the single most important reason for these problems, but chapters 1, 2 and 3 have highlighted other contributing factors such as disparities in regional growth rates, inflation coupled with an unresponsive tax base, unfortunate timing of benefit liberalizations, underfunding of the EB program and failure of states to act when fund balances were depleted. Because benefit outlays since 1969 have exceeded tax revenues by a wide margin, there has been a widespread loss of trust fund reserves, large scale borrowing and substantial debt accumulation. Total borrowing between 1972 and December 31, 1984 exceeded $23.4 billion.

Regional contrasts in economic performance have been particularly wide in the 1970s and early 1980s. States in the North have experienced especially high unemployment and low rates of economic growth since 1969. States in the South and West have fared much better. The geographic concentration of UI borrowing mirrors these regional contrasts. The North East region had especially high unemployment in the mid-1970s and accounted for about three-fifths of all UI loans needed between 1972 and 1979. Economic problems

165

were most serious in the North Central region in 1980-83 and about two-thirds of all loans in that period went to these states. Since unemployment and economic growth are factors beyond the control of the states, it may not be fair to hold these states fully liable for the UI debts which they have incurred. A detailed discussion of interstate cost sharing across UI programs lies beyond the scope of this volume. It is appropriate, however, to reemphasize here the sharp differences in unemployment and growth which have characterized state and regional economies of late.

In the early 1980s, the costs of UI debt rose substantially and debtor states have responded. The pace of debt repayments has increased and several states have enacted substantial revisions in their UI laws. Legislation to improve program solvency was passed in eight major debtor states between late 1982 and March 1984. Chapter 2 described these legislative packages. Tax increases plus benefit reductions from the legislation are estimated to improve solvency in these states by a total of $12 billion between 1983 and 1986. Employer and employee sacrifices constituted respectively 69 and 31 percent of the total change in solvency. The legislation was of such a scale that employers in these debtor states will realize almost $3 billion of UI tax savings during these years due to reduction, deferral and extension of payments for loan interest and FUT penalty taxes. The aggregate employer/worker sacrifice ratio changes from 69/31 to 59/41 when these savings are considered. The states have recently demonstrated an ability to improve solvency, and typically the legislation has involved multiple changes in both their tax and benefit provisions.

Trust fund rebuilding started to occur in 1984. At the beginning, the year net fund reserves across all state programs were –$5.7 billion. By the end of the year net reserves stood at about $2 billion, almost $8 billion higher. The small size of this net balance is another indicator of how widespread the loss of fund reserves has been.

While reserves remain low, UI programs will continue to be extremely vulnerable to the business cycle. In this situation, UI in the aggregate will behave more like a pay-as-you-go program rather than the automatic stabilizer it was originally intended to be. Faced with high costs of borrowing, the states would probably act again to raise taxes and reduce benefits shortly after the onset of another recession.

One obvious consequence of the recent state legislation is a reduction in the scale of UI relative to the overall economy. This reduction is apparent in several indicators, e.g., insured unemployment as a proportion of total unemployment and UI benefit payments as a percent of GNP. Payments for regular UI will be smaller, but with the virtual elimination of the EB program except for the most severe of recessions, the cutbacks in 1980-84 and in the future will be even larger in payments for long term unemployment. State UI programs will play a smaller future role in alleviating economic hardships due to unemployment than they did prior to 1980.

This report has focused on short run adaptations by the states to their funding problems. What about the future? One optimistic view of future trust fund developments is contained in a recent actuarial projection made by the Unemployment Insurance Service of the U.S. Department of Labor (1984b). They project net trust fund reserves to grow steadily after 1984 and to reach a total of $34 billion by the end of fiscal year 1989. Even if this comes to pass, the implied reserve ratio multiple for the U.S. as a whole will be roughly .75. Thus, twice this amount of reserves would be needed before the overall UI system of programs achieved the suggested minimum actuarial guideline of a 1.5 reserve ratio multiple. Even at the higher overall level for the U.S., the multiples for many state funds would still be lower than 1.5.

The $34 billion projected net trust fund balance may not be achieved by the end of fiscal 1989. The Labor Department's projection assumes that the average annual growth rate in real GNP will exceed 4 percent for the years 1985 through 1989. This rate of growth is higher than historic averages and implies that no recession will occur during the next five years. Should a recession recur before fund balances are restored there could be a repetition of the state-level adjustments described in chapter 2. Since many of the debtor states would probably still be in debt, they would experience the need for further tax increases and benefit reductions.

Probably the main conclusion of this volume should be that UI funding problems are likely to recur before the end of the present decade. In the short run, they will be avoided only if there is no recession. In the longer run, substantial fund building must take place. Indexing the taxable wage base would aid in fund building, but increases in UI tax rates are also required. A recent paper by Blaustein (1984) gives a vivid illustration as to the scale of tax increases that are required (to a U.S. average of 2 percent of total payrolls for three or four years) to achieve fund solvency. The only years when UI programs levied such high effective tax rates were before and during World War II.

To this author it seems unlikely that large scale UI tax increases (to even 1.5 percent of total payrolls) will take place. My judgment is that the states will not take the needed actions by themselves and that federal actions to promote trust fund accumulations are not likely, i.e., the promulgation of a federal solvency standard or the creation of new financial incentives to reward trust fund buildups. Given the observed responsiveness of state debt repayments in 1983 and 1984 to the interest rate costs of loans, it would seem that providing the states with positive financial incentives for fund building, i.e., a guarantee that a high interest rate would be paid on positive net reserve balances up to some level, would be an idea worth exploring. If substantial fund building does not occur, UI programs will remain exposed to the threat of recession and its two important consequences: the need to borrow to pay benefits and the need to enact additional legislation to improve program solvency.

APPENDIX
Summary Data for Selected State UI Programs

The tables on the following pages present summary data for 12 UI programs: the 10 states with the largest debts on December 31, 1983 (and discussed in chapter 2) plus California and Florida. These tables have a common format. Information on trust fund balances, loans, loan repayments and debt appear in columns 1-7. Benefit data appear in columns 8-11 while tax data appear in columns 12-15. All tables have annual data for the 14 years from 1970 to 1983. Most of the information appearing in the tables is based on data supplied by the Unemployment Insurance Service of the U.S. Department of Labor. Exact sources are listed in table A1. Note that the 1983 data are preliminary and subject to revision.

171

Table A1
Unemployment Insurance Trust Fund, Benefit and Tax Indicators for Pennsylvania, 1970-1983

Time period	Start-of-year reserve ratio multiple (1)	Start-of-year net reserves (2)	Total loans (3)	Interest-bearing loans (4)	Loan repayments (5)	Total end-of-year debt (6)	End-of-year interest-bearing debt (7)
1970	1.24	864	0	0	0	0	0
1971	1.17	852	0	0	0	0	0
1972	.98	743	0	0	0	0	0
1973	.70	590	0	0	0	0	0
1974	.64	595	0	0	0	0	0
1975	.52	529	174	0	0	174	0
1976	a	-86	379	0	0	553	0
1977	a	-535	373	0	0	926	0
1978	a	-902	261	0	0	1,187	0
1979	a	-997	35	0	0	1,222	0
1980	a	-1,091	222	0	57	1,387	0
1981	a	-1,243	305	0	126	1,566	0
1982	a	-1,297	816	651	237	2,145	545
1983	a	-2,145	1,244	1,244	772	2,617	1,151

Time period	Benefit indicators				Tax indicators			
	Benefits-to-total payroll (percent) (8)	Unemployment rate (percent) (9)	Ratio of insured-to-total unemployment (10)	Ratio of weekly benefits-to-weekly wages (11)	Taxes-to-total payroll (percent) (12)	Tax base per worker (13)	Taxable wages-to-total payroll (14)	Taxes-to-taxable wages (percent) (15)
U.S. 1970-79	1.15	6.2	.413	.364	1.00	4,320	.476	2.11
State 1970-79	1.63	6.3	.541	.406	1.08	4,440	.456	2.42
1970	.88	4.5	.489[b]	.361[b]	.66[b]	3,600[b]	.503[b]	1.31
1971	1.18	5.4	.536[b]	.361	.69[b]	3,600[b]	.481[b]	1.43
1972	1.37[b]	5.4	.528[b]	.424[b]	.77	4,200	.510	1.50
1973	1.12[b]	4.8	.490[b]	.424[b]	1.04[b]	4,200	.487	2.12[b]
1974	1.39[b]	5.1	.590[b]	.397[b]	1.14[b]	4,200	.448	2.54[b]
1975	2.86[b]	8.3	.674[b]	.421[b]	1.18[b]	4,200	.426	2.77[b]
1976	2.23[b]	7.9[b]	.563[b]	.423[b]	1.20[b]	4,200	.404	2.96[b]
1977	2.00[b]	7.7[b]	.539[b]	.419[b]	1.22[b]	4,200	.384	3.18[b]
1978	1.62[b]	6.9[b]	.504[b]	.421[b]	1.48[b]	6,000	.474	3.12[b]
1979	1.61[b]	6.9[b]	.498[b]	.409[b]	1.45[b]	6,000	.446	3.25[b]
1980	2.18[b]	7.8[b]	.559[b]	.422[b]	1.88[b]	6,300[b]	.418	4.49[b]
1981	1.89[b]	8.4[b]	.436[b]	.425[b]	1.67[b]	6,300[b]	.402	4.15[b]
1982	3.19[b]	10.9[b]	.488[b]	.468[b]	1.66[b]	6,600[b]	.400	4.14[b]
1983	2.73[b]	11.8[b]	.390[b]	.462[b]	1.88[b]	7,000	.403	4.65[b]

SOURCES: Most data taken from U.S. Department of Labor, *Unemployment Insurance Financial Data* (1984). Columns (3) and (9) based on unpublished U.S. Labor Department data. Columns (5), (10) and (15) estimated at The Urban Institute. Taxes in columns (12) and (15) include contributions from covered nonprofit organizations and governments. Data in columns (2)-(7) are measured in millions of dollars. Data for 1983 are preliminary.

a. Not shown because the net trust fund balance is negative.

b. State data for the year exceed the corresponding national data. For column (13) the comparative national indicator is the tax base for the Federal Unemployment Tax.

Table A2
Unemployment Insurance Trust Fund, Benefit and Tax Indicators for Illinois, 1970-1983

Time period	Start-of-year reserve ratio multiple (1)	Start-of-year net reserves (2)	Total loans (3)	Interest-bearing loans (4)	Loan repayments (5)	Total end-of-year debt (6)	End-of-year interest-bearing debt (7)
1970	1.17	500	0	0	0	0	0
1971	.90	401	0	0	0	0	0
1972	.60	280	0	0	0	0	0
1973	.50	258	0	0	0	0	0
1974	.75	424	0	0	0	0	0
1975	.81	507	69	0	0	69	0
1976	a	-31	446	0	0	515	0
1977	a	-505	243	0	0	759	0
1978	a	-717	188	0	0	946	0
1979	a	-604	0	0	0	946	0
1980	a	-460	38	0	0	984	0
1981	a	-918	487	0	66	1,405	0
1982	a	-1,381	843	488	181	2,069	442
1983	a	-2,069	1,174	1,174	835	2,423	928

Time period	Benefit indicators				Tax indicators			
	Benefits-to-total payroll (percent) (8)	Unemployment rate (percent) (9)	Ratio of insured-to-total unemployment (10)	Ratio of weekly benefits-to-weekly wages (11)	Taxes-to-total payroll (percent) (12)	Tax base per worker (13)	Taxable wages-to-total payroll (14)	Taxes-to-taxable wages (percent) (15)
U.S. 1970-79	1.15	6.2	.413	.364	1.00	4,320	.476	2.11
State 1970-79	1.07	5.4	.463	.360	.81	4,320	.414	1.94
1970	.69	3.6	.461[b]	.332	.22	3,000	.411	.54
1971	.85	5.1	.399	.316	.34	3,000	.384	.89
1972	.77	5.1	.355	.338	.66	4,200	.470	1.41
1973	.54	4.1	.337	.332	1.00[b]	4,200	.464	2.15[b]
1974	.68[b]	4.2	.425	.343	.85	4,200	.431	1.96
1975	1.78[b]	7.1	.602[b]	.368	.46	4,200	.396	1.18
1976	1.69[b]	6.5	.589[b]	.412[b]	.72	4,200	.375	1.92
1977	1.43[b]	6.2	.530[b]	.389[b]	1.07[b]	4,200	.363	2.95[b]
1978	1.14[b]	6.1	.455[b]	.380[b]	1.36[b]	6,000	.433	3.13[b]
1979	1.15[b]	5.5	.473[b]	.385[b]	1.38[b]	6,000	.421	3.28[b]
1980	1.98[b]	8.3[b]	.464[b]	.380[b]	1.36[b]	6,500[b]	.408	3.33[b]
1981	1.89[b]	8.5[b]	.417[b]	.410[b]	1.27[b]	6,500[b]	.387	3.29[b]
1982	2.42[b]	11.3[b]	.386[b]	.427[b]	1.45[b]	7,000[b]	.386	3.77[b]
1983	2.03[b]	11.4[b]	.322[b]	.424[b]	1.55[b]	8,000[b]	.411	3.77[b]

SOURCES: Most data taken from U.S. Department of Labor, *Unemployment Insurance Financial Data* (1984). Columns (3) and (9) based on unpublished U.S. Labor Department data. Columns (5), (10) and (15) estimated at The Urban Institute. Taxes in columns (12) and (15) include contributions from covered nonprofit organizations and governments. Data in columns (2)-(7) are measured in millions of dollars. Data for 1983 are preliminary.

a. Not shown because the net trust fund balance is negative.

b. State data for the year exceed the corresponding national data. For column (13) the comparative national indicator is the tax base for the Federal Unemployment Tax.

Table A3
Unemployment Insurance Trust Fund, Benefit and Tax Indicators for Michigan, 1970-1983

Time period	Start-of-year reserve ratio multiple (1)	Start-of-year net reserves (2)	Total loans (3)	Interest-bearing loans (4)	Loan repayments (5)	Total end-of-year debt (6)	End-of-year interest-bearing debt (7)
1970	854	630	0	0	0	0	0
1971	.67	491	0	0	0	0	0
1972	.40	312	0	0	0	0	0
1973	.44	383	0	0	0	0	0
1974	.57	564	0	0	0	0	0
1975	.38	395	326	0	0	326	0
1976	a	-286	245	0	0	571	0
1977	a	-391	53	0	0	624	0
1978	a	-273	0	0	0	624	0
1979	a	-7	0	0	624	0	0
1980	.07	112	842	0	0	842	0
1981	a	-633	233	0	0	1,075	0
1982	a	-1,066	1,182	694	71	2,186	623
1983	a	-2,186	790	790	653	2,322	800

176

Time period	Benefit indicators				Tax indicators			
	Benefits-to-total payroll (percent) (8)	Unemployment rate (percent) (9)	Ratio of insured-to-total unemployment (10)	Ratio of weekly benefits-to-weekly wages (11)	Taxes-to-total payroll (percent) (12)	Tax base per worker (13)	Taxable wages-to-total payroll (14)	Taxes-to-taxable wages (percent) (15)
U.S. 1970-79	1.15	6.2	.413	.364	1.00	4,320	.476	2.11
State 1970-79	1.41	793	.456	.336	1.22	4,680	.415	2.98
1970	1.43b	6.7b	.487b	.346	.61	3,600b	.456	1.34
1971	1.40b	7.6b	.455b	.336	.63	3,600b	.421	1.50b
1972	1.04b	7.0b	.398b	.319	1.31b	4,200	.444	2.96b
1973	.68	5.9b	.355	.296	1.25b	4,200	.419	2.99b
1974	1.65b	7.4b	.567b	.321	1.07b	4,200	.404	2.64b
1975	3.06b	12.5b	.525b	.372b	1.04b	4,200	.384	2.71b
1976	1.52b	9.4b	.433b	.366	1.47b	5,400b	.425	3.46b
1977	1.11	8.2b	.415b	.345	1.61b	5,400b	.398	4.03b
1978	.94b	6.9b	.441b	.322	1.65b	6,000	.408	4.03b
1979	1.31b	7.8b	.486b	.328	1.59b	6,000	.388	4.10b
1980	2.55b	12.4b	.534b	.316	1.38b	6,000	.368	3.76b
1981	1.98b	12.3b	.364	.368b	1.32b	6,000	.342	3.85b
1982	3.33b	15.5b	.349	.415b	1.31b	6,000	.332	3.93b
1983	1.88b	14.2b	.231	.398b	1.63b	8,000b	.393	4.37b

SOURCES: Most data taken from U.S. Department of Labor, *Unemployment Insurance Financial Data* (1984). Columns (3) and (9) based on unpublished U.S. Labor Department data. Columns (5), (10) and (15) estimated at The Urban Institute. Taxes in columns (12) and (15) include contributions from covered nonprofit organizations and governments. Data in columns (2)-(7) are measured in millions of dollars. Data for 1983 are preliminary.

a. Not shown because the net trust fund balance is negative.

b. State data for the year exceed the corresponding national data. For column (13) the comparative national indicator is the tax base for the Federal Unemployment Tax.

Table A4
Unemployment Insurance Trust Fund, Benefit and Tax Indicators for Ohio, 1970-1983

Time period	Start-of-year reserve ratio multiple (1)	Start-of-year net reserves (2)	Total loans (3)	Interest-bearing loans (4)	Loan repayments (5)	Total end-of-year debt (6)	End-of-year interest-bearing debt (7)
1970	1.27	703	0	0	0	0	0
1971	1.23	693	0	0	0	0	0
1972	1.07	619	0	0	0	0	0
1973	.96	626	0	0	0	0	0
1974	1.06	768	0	0	0	0	0
1975	.99	777	0	0	0	0	0
1976	.37	294	0	0	0	0	0
1977	.22	190	2	0	2	0	0
1978	.23	221	0	0	0	0	0
1979	.41	452	0	0	0	0	0
1980	.42	513	246	0	0	246	0
1981	a	-175	354	0	0	600	0
1982	a	-558	1,134	741	75	1,660	667
1983	a	-1,658	574	574	256	1,976	1,040

	Benefit indicators				Tax indicators			
Time period	Benefits-to-total payroll (percent) (8)	Unemployment rate (percent) (9)	Ratio of insured-to-total unemployment (10)	Ratio of weekly benefits-to-weekly wages (11)	Taxes-to-total payroll (percent) (12)	Tax base per worker (13)	Taxable wages-to-total payroll (14)	Taxes-to-taxable wages (percent) (15)
U.S. 1970-79	1.15	6.2	.413	.364	1.00	4,320	.476	2.11
State 1970-79	.87	6.1	.329	.372	738	4,320	.424	1.74
1970	.59	5.4[b]	.301	.324	.39	3,000	.417	.93
1971	.83	6.5[b]	.325	.313	.38	3,000	.393	.98
1972	.58	5.5	.264	.339	.52	4,200	.488	1.06
1973	.36	4.3	.237	.331	.72	4,200	.463	1.55
1974	.73	4.8	.364	.390[b]	.61	4,200	.438	1.40
1975	1.96	9.1[b]	.441	.400[b]	.56	4,200	.414	1.34
1976	1.04	7.8[b]	.310	.392[b]	.84	4,200	.387	2.18
1977	.91	6.5	.328	.395[b]	1.03	4,200	.363	2.84[b]
1978	.74	5.4	.326	.406[b]	1.22	6,000	.449	2.71
1979	.99[b]	5.9[b]	.391	.430[b]	1.04	6,000	.424	2.46
1980	2.09[b]	8.4[b]	.490[b]	.436[b]	.90	6,000	.401	2.24
1981	1.58[b]	9.6[b]	.346	.411[b]	.99	6,000	.372	2.67[b]
1982	2.74[b]	12.5[b]	.372	.439[b]	1.02	6,000	.359	2.83[b]
1983	1.75[b]	12.2[b]	.262	.416[b]	1.30	7,000	.387	3.35[b]

SOURCES: Most data taken from U.S. Department of Labor, *Unemployment Insurance Financial Data* (1984). Columns (3) and (9) based on unpublished U.S. Labor Department data. Columns (5), (10) and (15) estimated at The Urban Institute. Taxes in columns (12) and (15) include contributions from covered nonprofit organizations and governments. Data in columns (2)-(7) are measured in millions of dollars. Data for 1983 are preliminary.

a. Not shown because the net trust fund balance is negative.

b. State data for the year exceed the corresponding national data. For column (13) the comparative national indicator is the tax base for the Federal Unemployment Tax.

Table A5
Unemployment Insurance Trust Fund, Benefit and Tax Indicators for Texas, 1970-1983

Time period	Start-of-year reserve ratio multiple (1)	Start-of-year net reserves (2)	Total loans (3)	Interest-bearing loans (4)	Loan repayments (5)	Total end-of-year debt (6)	End-of-year interest-bearing debt (7)
1970	2.19	358	0	0	0	0	0
1971	1.94	337	0	0	0	0	0
1972	1.60	294	0	0	0	0	0
1973	1.33	289	0	0	0	0	0
1974	1.32	325	0	0	0	0	0
1975	1.20	343	0	0	0	0	0
1976	.72	231	0	0	0	0	0
1977	.55	205	0	0	0	0	0
1978	.59	249	0	0	0	0	0
1979	.68	346	0	0	0	0	0
1980	.66	397	0	0	0	0	0
1981	.40	275	0	0	0	0	0
1982	.31	254	143	143	0	143	143
1983	a	-142	661	661	119	685	685

	Benefit indicators				Tax indicators			
Time period	Benefits-to-total payroll (percent) (8)	Unemployment rate (percent) (9)	Ratio of insured-to-total unemployment (10)	Ratio of weekly benefits-to-weekly wages (11)	Taxes-to-total payroll (percent) (12)	Tax base per worker (13)	Taxable wages-to-total payroll (14)	Taxes-to-taxable wages (percent) (15)
U.S. 1970-79	1.15	6.2	.413	.364	1.00	4,320	.476	2.11
State 1970-79	.34	4.8	.194	.308	.27	4,320	.487	.56
1970	.35	4.4	.187	.306	.13	3,000	.477	.28
1971	.43	5.0	.196	.298	.13	3,000	.456b	.29
1972	.35	4.5	.160	.348	.26	4,200	.558b	.47
1973	.26	3.9	.164	.347	.34	4,200	.539b	.63
1974	.27	4.3	.180	.320	.27	4,200	.508b	.53
1975	.54	5.6	.270	.301	.18	4,200	.475b	.39
1976	.34	5.7	.191	.284	.29	4,200	.449	.64
1977	.30	5.3	.181	.272	.40	4,200	.424	.94
1978	.27	4.8	.192	.302	.43	6,000	.506b	.84
1979	.27	4.2	.223	.302	.31	6,000	.477b	.64
1980	.35	5.2	.222	.311	.16	6,000	.442	.35
1981	.28	5.3	.173	.324	.24	6,000	.410	.58
1982	.69	6.9	.241	.382b	.25	6,000	.383	.65
1983	1.01	8.0	.233	.400b	.41	7,000	.406	1.02

SOURCES: Most data taken from U.S. Department of Labor, *Unemployment Insurance Financial Data* (1984). Columns (3) and (9) based on unpublished U.S. Labor Department data. Columns (5), (10) and (15) estimated at The Urban Institute. Taxes in columns (12) and (15) include contributions from covered nonprofit organizations and governments. Data in columns (2)-(7) are measured in millions of dollars. Data for 1983 are preliminary.

a. Not shown because the net trust fund balance is negative.

b. State data for the year exceed the corresponding national data. For column (13) the comparative national indicator is the tax base for the Federal Unemployment Tax.

182

Table A6
Unemployment Insurance Trust Fund, Benefit and Tax Indicators for Wisconsin, 1970-1983

Time period	Start-of-year reserve ratio multiple (1)	Start-of-year net reserves (2)	Total loans (3)	Interest-bearing loans (4)	Loan repayments (5)	Total end-of-year debt (6)	End-of-year interest-bearing debt (7)
1970	2.40[b]	333	0	0	0	0	0
1971	2.36	322	0	0	0	0	0
1972	1.91	286	0	0	0	0	0
1973	1.63	278	0	0	0	0	0
1974	1.55	301	0	0	0	0	0
1975	1.47	316	0	0	0	0	0
1976	.44	121	0	0	0	0	0
1977	.54	165	0	0	0	0	0
1978	.68	231	0	0	0	0	0
1979	.93	362	0	0	0	0	0
1980	1.06	465	0	0	0	0	0
1981	.58	271	0	0	0	0	0
1982	.11	54	430	303	17	413	286
1983	a	-413	372	372	158	628	501

Time period	Benefit indicators				Tax indicators			
	Benefits-to-total payroll (percent) (8)	Unemployment rate (percent) (9)	Ratio of insured-to-total unemployment (10)	Ratio of weekly benefits-to-weekly wages (11)	Taxes-to-total payroll (percent) (12)	Tax base per worker (13)	Taxable wages-to-total payroll (14)	Taxes-to-taxable wages (percent) (15)
U.S. 1970-79	1.15	6.2	.413	.364	1.00	4,320	.476	2.11
State 1970-79	1.16	4.8	.470	.415	1.07	4,800	.479	2.22
1970	1.10[b]	4.0	.507[b]	.396[b]	.73[b]	3,600[b]	.515[b]	1.42[b]
1971	1.26[b]	4.5	.502[b]	.397[b]	.64	3,600[b]	.465[b]	1.39
1972	.96	4.3	.449[b]	.393[b]	.76	4,200	.500	1.53
1973	.74	4.0	.376[b]	.413[b]	.81	4,200	.481	1.69
1974	.92	4.5	.414	.412[b]	.89	4,200	.456	1.96
1975	2.12[b]	6.9	.610[b]	.436[b]	.87	4,200	.429	2.02[b]
1976	1.31	5.6	.528[b]	.435[b]	1.39[b]	6,000[b]	.520[b]	2.68[b]
1977	1.16	4.9	.504[b]	.420[b]	1.56[b]	6,000[b]	.498[b]	2.89[b]
1978	.96[b]	5.1	.391[b]	.421[b]	1.63[b]	6,000	.474	3.43
1979	1.11[b]	4.5	.508[b]	.427[b]	1.44[b]	6,000	.448	3.22[b]
1980	2.17[b]	7.2[b]	.586[b]	.448[b]	1.14[b]	6,000	.419	2.72[b]
1981	1.91[b]	7.8[b]	.471[b]	.436[b]	.96	6,000	.392	2.44[b]
1982	2.83[b]	10.7[b]	.411[b]	.460[b]	1.00	6,000	.378	2.65[b]
1983	2.11[b]	10.4[b]	.338[b]	.451[b]	1.25[b]	8,000[b]	.454[b]	2.75

SOURCES: Most data taken from U.S. Department of Labor, *Unemployment Insurance Financial Data* (1984). Columns (3) and (9) based on unpublished U.S. Labor Department data. Columns (5), (10) and (15) estimated at The Urban Institute. Taxes in columns (12) and (15) include contributions from covered nonprofit organizations and governments. Data in columns (2)-(7) are measured in millions of dollars. Data for 1983 are preliminary.

a. Not shown because the net trust fund balance is negative.

b. State data for the year exceed the corresponding national data. For column (13) the comparative national indicator is the tax base for the Federal Unemployment Tax.

Table A7
Unemployment Insurance Trust Fund, Benefit and Tax Indicators for Louisiana, 1970-1983

Time period	Start-of-year reserve ratio multiple (1)	Start-of-year net reserves (2)	Total loans (3)	Interest-bearing loans (4)	Loan repayments (5)	Total end-of-year debt (6)	End-of-year interest-bearing debt (7)
1970	1.74	163	0	0	0	0	0
1971	1.49	146	0	0	0	0	0
1972	1.23	128	0	0	0	0	0
1973	.98	118	0	0	0	0	0
1974	.89	119	0	0	0	0	0
1975	.93	138	0	0	0	0	0
1976	.81	141	0	0	0	0	0
1977	.83	165	0	0	0	0	0
1978	.56	125	0	0	0	0	0
1979	.46	124	0	0	0	0	0
1980	.77	238	0	0	0	0	0
1981	.63	223	0	0	0	0	0
1982	.51	210	102	102	0	102	102
1983	a	-102	427	427	53	476	476

185

Time period	Benefit indicators				Tax indicators			
	Benefits-to-total payroll (percent) (8)	Unemployment rate (percent) (9)	Ratio of insured-to-total unemployment (10)	Ratio of weekly benefits-to-weekly wages (11)	Taxes-to-total payroll (percent) (12)	Tax base per worker (13)	Taxable wages-to-total payroll (14)	Taxes-to-taxable wages (percent) (15)
U.S. 1970-79	1.15	6.2	.413	.364	1.00	4,320	.476	2.11
State 1970-79	1.02	7.1	.313	.365	.97	4,320	.487	2.01
1970	1.12[b]	6.7[b]	.326	.329	.63	3,000	.477	1.31
1971	1.14	7.4[b]	.287	.335	.71[b]	3,000	.449	1.58[b]
1972	.93	7.7[b]	.238	.352	.62	4,200	.559[b]	1.10
1973	.91[b]	6.8[b]	.280	.366[b]	.87	4,200	.540[b]	1.60
1974	.91	7.1[b]	.302	.349	1.11[b]	4,200	.515[b]	2.17[b]
1975	1.19	7.4	.403	.346	1.18[b]	4,200	.464[b]	2.55[b]
1976	.98	6.8	.366	.355	1.14	4,200	.446	2.56[b]
1977	1.25[b]	7.0	.371	.404[b]	.96	4,200	.425	2.26
1978	.90	7.0[b]	.282	.413[b]	.89	6,000	.514[b]	1.74
1979	.89	6.7[b]	.277	.403[b]	1.58[b]	6,000	.483[b]	3.27[b]
1980	1.13	6.7	.305	.396[b]	.97	6,000	.451[b]	2.15
1981	1.07	8.4[b]	.260	.394[b]	.90	6,000	.418	2.15
1982	2.23[b]	10.3[b]	.361	.444[b]	.84	6,000	.380	2.21
1983	2.29[b]	11.7[b]	.352[b]	.385[b]	NA	7,000	NA	3.31[b]

SOURCES: Most data taken from U.S. Department of Labor, *Unemployment Insurance Financial Data* (1984). Columns (3) and (9) based on unpublished U.S. Labor Department data. Columns (5), (10) and (15) estimated at The Urban Institute. Taxes in columns (12) and (15) include contributions from covered nonprofit organizations and governments. Data in columns (2)-(7) are measured in millions of dollars. Data for 1983 are preliminary.

a. Not shown because the net trust fund balance is negative.

b. State data for the year exceed the corresponding national data. For column (13) the comparative national indicator is the tax base for the Federal Unemployment Tax.

NA = Not available.

Table A8

Unemployment Insurance Trust Fund, Benefit and Tax Indicators for New Jersey, 1970-1983

Time period	Start-of-year reserve ratio multiple (1)	Start-of-year net reserves (2)	Total loans (3)	Interest-bearing loans (4)	Loan repayments (5)	Total end-of-year debt (6)	End-of-year interest-bearing debt (7)
1970	1.22	483	0	0	0	0	0
1971	1.05	448	0	0	0	0	0
1972	.57	225	0	0	0	0	0
1973	.28	138	0	0	0	0	0
1974	.29	138	0	0	0	0	0
1975	.07	41	352	0	0	352	0
1976	a	-348	145	0	0	497	0
1977	a	-482	142	0	0	639	0
1978	a	-570	96	0	40	695	0
1979	a	-547	0	0	43	652	0
1980	a	-507	0	0	0	652	0
1981	a	-496	0	0	39	612	0
1982	a	-422	0	0	92	521	0
1983	a	-423	79	79	177	422	0

Time period	Benefit indicators				Tax indicators			
	Benefits-to-total payroll (percent) (8)	Unemployment rate (percent) (9)	Ratio of insured-to-total unemployment (10)	Ratio of weekly benefits-to-weekly wages (11)	Taxes-to-total payroll (percent) (12)	Tax base per worker (13)	Taxable wages-to-total payroll (14)	Taxes-to-taxable wages (percent) (15)
U.S. 1970-79	1.15	6.2	.413	.364	1.00	4,320	.476	2.11
State 1970-79	1.91	7.2	.540	.369	1.59	4,860	.464	3.44
1970	1.49[b]	4.6	.631[b]	.386[b]	1.13[b]	3,600[b]	.481[b]	2.35[b]
1971	1.95[b]	5.7	.656[b]	.397[b]	1.09[b]	3,600[b]	.458[b]	2.38[b]
1972	1.89[b]	5.8[b]	.575[b]	NA	1.23[b]	4,200	.487	2.52[b]
1973	1.55[b]	5.6[b]	.561[b]	.381[b]	1.64[b]	4,200	.467	3.52[b]
1974	1.97[b]	6.3[b]	.646[b]	.369[b]	1.60[b]	4,200	.426	3.76[b]
1975	2.89[b]	10.2[b]	.537[b]	.366	1.67[b]	4,800[b]	.451	3.70[b]
1976	2.16[b]	10.4[b]	.409[b]	.354	1.77[b]	5,400[b]	.469[b]	3.77[b]
1977	1.90[b]	9.4[b]	.396[b]	.356	1.94[b]	5,800[b]	.469[b]	4.13[b]
1978	1.70[b]	7.2[b]	.473[b]	.357	1.94[b]	6,200[b]	.469	4.15[b]
1979	1.63[b]	6.9[b]	.512[b]	.352	1.90[b]	6,600[b]	.464	4.10[b]
1980	1.81[b]	7.2[b]	.527[b]	.348	1.77[b]	6,900[b]	.447	3.96[b]
1981	1.61[b]	7.3	.482[b]	.338	1.69[b]	7,500[b]	.444[b]	3.80[b]
1982	1.85[b]	9.0	.427[b]	.353	1.65[b]	8,200[b]	.442[b]	3.73[b]
1983	1.45[b]	7.8	.393[b]	.351	1.60[b]	8,800[b]	.445[b]	3.60[b]

SOURCES: Most data taken from U.S. Department of Labor, *Unemployment Insurance Financial Data* (1984). Columns (3) and (9) based on unpublished U.S. Labor Department data. Columns (5), (10) and (15) estimated at The Urban Institute. Taxes in columns (12) and (15) include contributions from covered nonprofit organizations and governments. Data in columns (2)-(7) are measured in millions of dollars. Data for 1983 are preliminary.

a. Not shown because the net trust fund balance is negative.

b. State data for the year exceed the corresponding national data. For column (13) the comparative national indicator is the tax base for the Federal Unemployment Tax.

NA = Not available.

Table A9

Unemployment Insurance Trust Fund, Benefit and Tax Indicators for Minnesota, 1970-1983

Time period	Start-of-year reserve ratio multiple (1)	Start-of-year net reserves (2)	Total loans (3)	Interest-bearing loans (4)	Loan repayments (5)	Total end-of-year debt (6)	End-of-year interest-bearing debt (7)
1970	1.11	120	0	0	0	0	0
1971	1.04	119	0	0	0	0	0
1972	.76	92	0	0	0	0	0
1973	.61	82	0	0	0	0	0
1974	.61	92	0	0	0	0	0
1975	.45	76	47	0	0	47	0
1976	a	-35	76	0	0	123	0
1977	a	-19	49	0	0	172	0
1978	a	-89	0	0	0	172	0
1979	a	8	0	0	172	0	0
1980	.22	70	28	0	0	28	0
1981	a	-13	86	0	0	114	0
1982	a	-84	193	115	19	288	96
1983	a	-288	241	241	178	352	183

Time period	Benefit indicators				Tax indicators			
	Benefits-to-total payroll (percent) (8)	Unemployment rate (percent) (9)	Ratio of insured-to-total unemployment (10)	Ratio of weekly benefits-to-weekly wages (11)	Taxes-to-total payroll (percent) (12)	Tax base per worker (13)	Taxable wages-to-total payroll (14)	Taxes-to-taxable wages (percent) (15)
U.S. 1970-79	1.15	6.2	.413	.364	1.00	4,320	.476	2.11
State 1970-79	1.01	4.7	.437	.386	.92	5,750	.538	1.72
1970	.78	4.2	.384	.359[b]	.68[b]	4,800[b]	.594[b]	1.14
1971	.98	4.4	.451[b]	.345	.59	4,800[b]	.563[b]	1.04
1972	.87	4.3	.440[b]	.356	.74	4,800[b]	.549[b]	1.36
1973	.76	4.5	.365	.353	.81	4,800[b]	.524[b]	1.55
1974	1.03	4.3	.484[b]	.389[b]	.87	4,800[b]	.495[b]	1.76
1975	1.67	5.9	.567[b]	.378[b]	.81	4,800[b]	.476[b]	1.69
1976	1.38	5.9	.456[b]	.410[b]	1.00	6,200[b]	.534[b]	1.87
1977	1.10	5.1	.435[b]	.403[b]	1.26	7,000[b]	.552[b]	2.29
1978	.77	3.8	.411[b]	.430[b]	1.31	7,500[b]	.551[b]	2.38
1979	.78	4.2	.379	.433[b]	1.18	8,000[b]	.542[b]	2.17
1980	.78[b]	5.9	.405	.444[b]	1.03	8,000[b]	.508[b]	2.03
1981	1.51[b]	5.5	.401[b]	.435[b]	.93	8,000[b]	.477[b]	1.94
1982	1.28[b]	7.8	.401[b]	.437[b]	.97	8,300[b]	.461[b]	2.11
1983	1.89[b]	8.2	.283	.422[b]	1.11	9,000[b]	.461[b]	2.41

SOURCES: Most data taken from U.S. Department of Labor, *Unemployment Insurance Financial Data* (1984). Columns (3) and (9) based on unpublished U.S. Labor Department data. Columns (5), (10) and (15) estimated at The Urban Institute. Taxes in columns (12) and (15) include contributions from covered nonprofit organizations and governments. Data in columns (2)-(7) are measured in millions of dollars. Data for 1983 are preliminary.

a. Not shown because the net trust fund balance is negative.

b. State data for the year exceed the corresponding national data. For column (13) the comparative national indicator is the tax base for the Federal Unemployment Tax.

Table A10
Unemployment Insurance Trust Fund, Benefit and Tax Indicators for West Virginia, 1970-1983

Time period	Start-of-year reserve ratio multiple (1)	Start-of-year net reserves (2)	Total loans (3)	Interest-bearing loans (4)	Loan repayments (5)	Total end-of-year debt (6)	End-of-year interest-bearing debt (7)
1970	1.59	102	0	0	0	0	0
1971	1.55	108	0	0	0	0	0
1972	1.48	111	0	0	0	0	0
1973	1.23	108	0	0	0	0	0
1974	1.20	114	0	0	0	0	0
1975	1.10	116	0	0	0	0	0
1976	.65	78	0	0	0	0	0
1977	.54	72	0	0	0	0	0
1978	.43	64	0	0	0	0	0
1979	.34	57	0	0	0	0	0
1980	.21	39	47	0	0	0	0
1981	a	-44	53	0	0	100	0
1982	a	-71	45	40	0	144	39
1983	a	-144	152	152	8	288	192

Time period	Benefit indicators				Tax indicators			
	Benefits-to-total payroll (percent) (8)	Unemployment rate (percent) (9)	Ratio of insured-to-total unemployment (10)	Ratio of weekly benefits-to-weekly wages (11)	Taxes-to-total payroll (percent) (12)	Tax base per worker (13)	Taxable wages-to-total payroll (14)	Taxes-to-taxable wages (percent) (15)
U.S. 1970-79	1.15	6.2	.413	.364	1.00	4,320	.476	2.11
State 1970-79	.93	NA	NA	.286	.74	4,440	.469	1.61
1970	.59	NA	NA	.238	.63	3,600[b]	.513[b]	1.23
1971	.72	NA	NA	.220	.63	3,600[b]	.496[b]	1.27
1972	.76	NA	NA	.274	.55	4,200	.528[b]	1.05
1973	.68	NA	NA	.282	.70	4,200	.508[b]	1.38
1974	.74	NA	NA	.279	.60	4,200	.479[b]	1.26
1975	1.31	NA	NA	.309	.51	4,200	.427	1.20
1976	.93	7.5	.387	.282	.82	4,200	.413	1.98
1977	.99	7.1	.420[b]	.290	.83	4,200	.403	1.07
1978	1.15[b]	6.3[b]	.481	.319	1.00	6,000	.479	2.09
1979	1.45[b]	6.7[b]	.474[b]	.362	1.16	6,000	.448	2.59
1980	2.17[b]	9.4[b]	.432	.383	1.09	6,000	.418	2.60[b]
1981	1.96[b]	10.7[b]	.414[b]	.366	1.72[b]	8,000[b]	.484[b]	3.55[b]
1982	3.01[b]	13.9[b]	.386[b]	.400[b]	2.13[b]	8,000[b]	.466[b]	4.56[b]
1983	3.57[b]	18.0[b]	.305	.434[b]	1.95[b]	8,000[b]	.454[b]	4.29[b]

SOURCES: Most data taken from U.S. Department of Labor, *Unemployment Insurance Financial Data* (1984). Columns (3) and (9) based on unpublished U.S. Labor Department data. Columns (5), (10) and (15) estimated at The Urban Institute. Taxes in columns (12) and (15) include contributions from covered nonprofit organizations and governments. Data in columns (2)-(7) are measured in millions of dollars. Data for 1983 are preliminary.

a. Not shown because the net trust fund balance is negative.

b. State data for the year exceed the corresponding national data. For column (13) the comparative national indicator is the tax base for the Federal Unemployment Tax.

NA = Not available.

Table A11
Unemployment Insurance Trust Fund, Benefit and Tax Indicators for California, 1970-1983

Time period	Start-of-year reserve ratio multiple (1)	Start-of-year net reserves (2)	Total loans (3)	Interest-bearing loans (4)	Loan repayments (5)	Total end-of-year debt (6)	End-of-year interest-bearing debt (7)
1970	1.43	1,305	0	0	0	0	0
1971	1.29	1,219	0	0	0	0	0
1972	.93	905	0	0	0	0	0
1973	.90	975	0	0	0	0	0
1974	1.02	1,221	0	0	0	0	0
1975	.87	1,153	0	0	0	0	0
1976	.38	641	0	0	0	0	0
1977	.38	641	0	0	0	0	0
1978	.58	1,088	0	0	0	0	0
1979	.80	1,756	0	0	0	0	0
1980	1.07	2,738	0	0	0	0	0
1981	1.08	3,088	0	0	0	0	0
1982	1.05	3,353	0	0	0	0	0
1983	.80	2,708	0	0	0	0	0

193

Time period	Benefit indicators				Tax indicators			
	Benefits-to-total payroll (percent) (8)	Unemployment rate (percent) (9)	Ratio of insured-to-total unemployment (10)	Ratio of weekly benefits-to-weekly wages (11)	Taxes-to-total payroll (percent) (12)	Tax base per worker (13)	Taxable wages-to-total payroll (14)	Taxes-to-taxable wages (percent) (15)
U.S. 1970-79	1.15	6.2	.413	.364	1.00	4,320	.476	2.11
State 1970-79	1.38	7.9	.405	.330	1.46	5,040	.490	2.97
1970	1.58[b]	7.3[b]	.454[b]	.351	1.22[b]	3,800[b]	.511[b]	2.38[b]
1971	1.72[b]	8.8[b]	.402	.341	1.06[b]	3,800[b]	.483[b]	2.19[b]
1972	1.27[b]	7.6[b]	.369	.333	1.36[b]	4,200	.499	2.72[b]
1973	1.12[b]	7.0[b]	.365	.339	1.45[b]	4,200	.481	3.01[b]
1974	1.41[b]	7.3[b]	.419	.347	1.24[b]	4,200	.457	2.70[b]
1975	2.12[b]	9.9[b]	.449	.334	1.30[b]	4,200	.424	3.05[b]
1976	1.54[b]	9.2[b]	.395	.335	1.83[b]	7,000[b]	.560[b]	3.26[b]
1977	1.26[b]	8.2[b]	.377	.319	1.90[b]	7,000[b]	.551[b]	3.45[b]
1978	1.03[b]	7.1[b]	.400[b]	.310	1.68[b]	6,000	.482	3.49[b]
1979	.79	6.2[b]	.417[b]	.292	1.55[b]	6,000	.454	3.41[b]
1980	1.11	6.8	.472[b]	.295	1.18[b]	6,000	.420	2.82[b]
1981	1.03	7.4	.429[b]	.289	.99	6,000	.392	2.51[b]
1982	1.55	9.9[b]	.427[b]	.291	1.00	6,000	.363	2.75[b]
1983	1.36	9.7[b]	.385[b]	.296	1.01	7,000	.388	2.60

SOURCES: Most data taken from U.S. Department of Labor, *Unemployment Insurance Financial Data* (1984). Columns (3) and (9) based on unpublished U.S. Labor Department data. Columns (5), (10) and (15) estimated at The Urban Institute. Taxes in columns (12) and (15) include contributions from covered nonprofit organizations and governments. Data in columns (2)–(7) are measured in millions of dollars. Data for 1983 are preliminary.

a. Not shown because the net trust fund balance is negative.

b. State data for the year exceed the corresponding national data. For column (13) the comparative national indicator is the tax base for the Federal Unemployment Tax.

Table A12

Unemployment Insurance Trust Fund, Benefit and Tax Indicators for Florida, 1970-1983

Time period	Start-of-year reserve ratio multiple (1)	Start-of-year net reserves (2)	Total loans (3)	Interest-bearing loans (4)	Loan repayments (5)	Total end-of-year debt (6)	End-of-year interest-bearing debt (7)
1970	2.42	256	0	0	0	0	0
1971	2.30	268	0	0	0	0	0
1972	2.15	276	0	0	0	0	0
1973	1.78	302	0	0	0	0	0
1974	1.69	344	0	0	0	0	0
1975	1.51	326	0	0	0	0	0
1976	.23	80	10	0	10	0	0
1977	.07	24	32	0	32	0	0
1978	.27	111	0	0	0	0	0
1979	.83	403	0	0	0	0	0
1980	1.16	665	0	0	0	0	0
1981	1.21	813	0	0	0	0	0
1982	1.20	919	0	0	0	0	0
1983	1.05	866	0	0	0	0	0

	Benefit indicators				Tax indicators			
Time period	Benefits-to-total payroll (percent) (8)	Unemployment rate (percent) (9)	Ratio of insured-to-total unemployment (10)	Ratio of weekly benefits-to-weekly wages (11)	Taxes-to-total payroll (percent) (12)	Tax base per worker (13)	Taxable wages-to-total payroll (14)	Taxes-to-taxable wages (percent) (15)
U.S. 1970-79	1.15	6.2	.413	.364	1.00	4,320	.476	2.11
State 1970-79	.61	6.5	.258	.328	.69	4,320	.517	1.34
1970	.36	4.3	.265	.277	.35	3,000	.503[b]	.69
1971	.44	4.9	.282	.295	.38	3,000	.480[b]	.79
1972	.27	5.1	.213	.318	.37	4,200	.549[b]	.67
1973	.22	4.3	.204	.322	.36	4,200	.538[b]	.66
1974	.57	6.2[b]	.263	.403[b]	.37	4,200	.542[b]	.69
1975	1.62	1.07[b]	.343	.358	.49	4,200	.504[b]	.97
1976	1.08	9.0[b]	.302	.351	.92	4,200	.492[b]	1.87
1977	.74	8.2[b]	.256	.329	1.18	4,200	.472[b]	2.49
1978	.42	6.6[b]	.225	.319	1.44[b]	6,000	.561[b]	2.56
1979	.36	6.0[b]	.226	.305	1.08	6,000	.529[b]	2.03
1980	.42	5.9	.257	.311	.63	6,000	.502[b]	1.25
1981	.41	6.8	.198	.309	.46	6,000	.470[b]	.98
1982	.75	8.2	.234	.340	.42	6,000	.441[b]	.96
1983	.61	8.6	.179	.332	.52	7,000	.468[b]	1.11

SOURCES: Most data taken from U.S. Department of Labor, *Unemployment Insurance Financial Data* (1984). Columns (3) and (9) based on unpublished U.S. Labor Department data. Columns (5), (10) and (15) estimated at The Urban Institute. Taxes in columns (12) and (15) include contributions from covered nonprofit organizations and governments. Data in columns (2)-(7) are measured in millions of dollars. Data for 1983 are preliminary.

a. Not shown because the net trust fund balance is negative.

b. State data for the year exceed the corresponding national data. For column (13) the comparative national indicator is the tax base for the Federal Unemployment Tax.

References

Arthur Anderson and Co., "Reference Paper One: Summary of U.C. Fund Analysis and Task Force Proposal," Prepaid for the Governor's Task Force on Emergency Jobs and the Unemployment Trust Fund (Austin, TX: Arthur Anderson and Co., May 1983).

Becker, Joseph, S.J., *Unemployment Insurance Financing* (Washington, DC: American Enterprise Institute, 1981).

Blaustein, Saul, "Recent Changes in Michigan's Unemployment Insurance Laws," W. E. Upjohn Institute, Mimeo (April 21, 1981).

Blaustein, Saul, "State Unemployment Insurance Fund Adequacy: Past and Present Perspectives," Paper presented at the Industrial Relations Research Association Annual Meetings, Dallas, Texas (December 29, 1984).

Blaustein, Saul, *Unemployment Insurance Fund Insolvency and Debt in Michigan* (Kalamazoo, MI: W. E. Upjohn Institute, 1982).

Burtless, Gary, "Why is Insured Unemployment So Low?" *Brookings Papers on Economic Activity* (1983:1), pp. 225-253.

Hemmerly, Jim, "1983-1985 Cost Estimates," Introffice Communication, Ohio Bureau of Employment Services, Columbus, Ohio (June 28, 1983).

Hight, Joseph, "Trends in Unemployment Insurance Wage Replacement, 1950 to 1977," in National Commission on Unemployment Compensation, *Unemployment Compensation: Studies and Research, Vol. 1* (Washington, DC: National Commission on Unemployment Compensation, 1980), pp. 215-222.

Hobbie, Richard, "Unemployment Compensation: FY84 Budget," Congressional Research Service Issue Brief No. IB83036 (Washington, DC: Library of Congress, April 1983).

Hobbie, Richard, "Unemployment Insurance: Financial Trouble in the Trust Fund," Congressional Research Service Issue Brief No. IB79098 (Washington, DC: Library of Congress, September 1982).

McCormick, Patricia, "A Jobless Fund in Crisis," *Pennsylvania Economy* (August 1983), pp. 8-13.

Mackin, Paul, *Benefit Financing in Unemployment Insurance: A Problem of Balancing Responsibilities* (Kalamazoo, MI: W. E. Upjohn Institute, 1978).

Myers, Robert, *Social Security,* Second Edition, Published for McCahan Foundation (Homewood, IL: Richard D. Irwin, 1981).

Perry, George, "Changing Labor Markets and Inflation," *Brookings Papers on Economic Activity* (1970:3), pp. 411-441.

Runner, Diana, "Changes in Unemployment Insurance Legislation During 1983," *Monthly Labor Review* (February 1984), pp. 46-54.

Runner, Diana, "Legislative Revisions of Unemployment Insurance in 1980," *Monthly Labor Review* (January 1981), pp. 35-39.

Runner, Diana, "Unemployment Insurance Laws: Changes Enacted During 1981," *Monthly Labor Review* (February 1982), pp. 16-23.

State of Illinois, "General Summary Impact of Public Act 83-1: 1983 Unemployment Insurance Program Reforms" (Springfield, IL: State of Illinois, 1983).

State of Michigan, "Summary of 1982 Amendments to the Michigan Employment Security Act" (Detroit, MI: Michigan Employment Security Commission, January 1983).

State of Pennsylvania, Department of Labor and Industry, "1983 Actuarial Evaluation: Financial Operations of the Pennsylvania Unemployment Compensation Program" (Harrisburg, PA: State of Pennsylvania, December 1983).

State of Texas, "Governor's Task Force on Emergency Jobs and the Unemployment Trust Fund" (Austin, TX: State of Texas, May 1983).

State of Wisconsin, "Wisconsin's Unemployment Compensation Law 1983 Amendments" (Madison, WI: State of Wisconsin, May 1983).

Texas Research League, "Unemployment Compensation Tax Revisions-Decreasing the Tax Increase," *Texas Research League Analysis* (October 1982), pp. 5-8.

Texas Research League, "UC Trust Fund Fix by HB896," *Texas Research League Analysis* (July 1983), pp. 1-4.

U.S. Department of Labor, Employment and Training Administration, *Unemployment Insurance Financial Data,* ET Handbook 394 (Washington, DC: U.S. Department of Labor, 1984a).

U.S. Department of Labor, Unemployment Insurance Service, "UI Outlook: FY1984 Budget—Midsession Review," Division of Actuarial Services (August 10, 1984b).

U.S. Executive Office of the President, *Economic Report of the President, 1984* (Washington, DC: GPO, 1984).

Vroman, Wayne, "The Reagan Administration and Unemployment Insurance," The Urban Institute (March 1984).